The Business School

Approach to

Writing Your Novel

by

Michael Davies

The Business School Approach To Writing Your Novel

For information address: mickiedaltonbooks@lycos.com

First Printing 2009
ISBN: 978-0-9818087-8-9

Second Edition Printed July, 2010
ISBN: 978-9808164-0-2

First Printed In Australia

**Published by The Mickie Dalton Foundation
Kempsey, NSW
Australia**

www.mickiedaltonfoundation.com

Dedicated to the young people at St. Joseph's Catholic High School in Albion Park, NSW who took me along the journey that led us to "The Mickie Dalton Trilogy" and beyond

James Arblaster   Catherine Fitzpatrick
Paul Foster   Melissa Foye
James Goddard   Michael Guinery
Evan Hayes   Gabrielle McCann
Vincent Muller   Adam Piovarchy
Alicia Quinn   Michael Robson
Samuel Troutman   TJ Viney
Sebastian Wattam

And with huge thanks also to the members of the South West Rocks Writing Class and the members of the classes of the Camp Creative courses that I taught in 2013 and 2104, all of whom helped me fine tune this methodology

Other Books by Michael Davies

The Nightmares of God
The Janus Conspiracy
Accounts of a Killing
A Friendly Killing
Dreamkill
Ready, Steady, KILL!

For the Young Adults (12-18)
The Many Worlds of Mickie Dalton
The Many Galaxies of Mickie Dalton
The Many Universes of Mickie Dalton

For the 8-12 age group
The Julie Malloy Gang and the Smugglers
The Mysterious Recorder and the Door to Elsewhere
The Quest for the Locket
The Secret of Yuri Kirilenko
The Secret of Charlotte's Cello
The United Nations and the Extra-Terrestrial
The Star of the Yshan Kings
The War of the Yshan Empire
The Star of the New Yshan Empire
The Red Fog of Time
Prisoners of the Picture

For the Little Ones (3-5)
Mary's World

Table of Contents

Introduction

At the grand old age of 35, I walked away from the IT industry after twelve years of mixed success and failure, taking the standard path of baby programmer at which I had been quite mediocre, through systems analyst (pretty good) to management (adequate) and entered business school for the two year MBA program at the University of Western Ontario in London, Canada.

As it still does, UWO's Richard Ivey School of Business maintained a close working relationship with the Harvard Business School, with joint committees coordinating grading, methodologies, case development etc., and many of the professors of both schools had done their doctorates at one or the other.

One standard of the case study methodology was that students formed working groups, usually three to five in each and we developed tightly knit, supportive relationships with the members of our group. Each day, we would be given a business case to analyse for each topic of the day, such as HR, Finance, Marketing, Operations, etc., and be prepared to present the case to the class at the next session of that topic. Regularly, a major case would be given on the Friday and a complete report had to be submitted to a locked box by the Sunday afternoon. This normally required working long hours, often till the early hours of the morning on both Friday and Saturday nights.

The first time this happened was an enormous shock to me. Regular practice was to take the case away and work on it alone for two or three hours, then meet with the group in the evening. I remember how confidently I took the case home to my apartment and studied it carefully, analyzed it, extracted all the key points, developed a conclusion and a recommended solution to the problem and set off to Sue's apartment (she had the best and biggest apartment!) to join Richard and Moe to continue. I had the thing beaten, I was certain. After all, I was 35, I'd had 11 years of commercial Information Technology experience, I'd already designed finance, accounting, operations, real estate and other systems, the other three were in their mid-twenties, there was nothing these kids nor those youthful professors could show me.

That pleasant delusion lasted for five minutes after we started to compare notes. The others had seen aspects of the case I had not seen, suggested approaches I'd never considered and recommended solutions quite new to me. To be fair to myself, I think all of us had the same surprise, but I was quite shaken to realise how shallow my thinking had been. In the end, we produced what to us was a deeply thought-out analysis, with my skills put to use in developing a computer model that allowed flexible decision-making and some good conclusions. Actually, it was quite good and we all got high grades, but this was just the start.

The second shock was when the whole class got together and the professor ran his analysis, covering three large whiteboards with notes. If we thought we had done an in-depth analysis, we were rapidly re-educated. It was breath-taking how the process of evaluation, analysis and development was laid out, enhanced, developed and completed. I learned then why the blackboard, now whiteboard is considered the finest development and problem-solving tool in all fields of business, science, art, etc. My group began using the whiteboard for all our analyses and I found the new technique quite exhilarating.

On graduation and return to the business world, now as a business consultant, I used the same approach with my clients and have done so ever since for all sorts of issues where problem solving or solution designs were required.

Then came the Mickie Dalton project.

I'd begun writing some 20 years earlier, with my fifth completed novel finally seeming worthy of submission to literary agents. The hobby had been a wonderful way of relaxing from the increasing pressures and responsibilities I was experiencing with more senior positions in the USA and Canada involving much international travel. That fifth novel had eventually been published and I had experienced that incredible moment of opening the package and seeing my first book in print.

It would be some years before it happened again. But on returning home to Australia, I began writing the first of what would be a trilogy for the "Young Adult" population of 12-18 year-olds, and completed it all on my own. But I had already been considering how much better the task would be if I could work with a group of the target readership and get their input.

Very fortunately, I met a drama teacher, Jennifer Rush who liked the idea, introduced me to the Head of English at her school, Andrew Rout who also liked the idea and the project started with fifteen exceptional young Grade 8 students.

I fell into my customary role of facilitating a brainstorming session at the whiteboard and the results were astonishing. After three terms we had three books and these have been quite successful.

I have since used this approach with seniors, with adults and with primary school children and the results continue to startle me. Starting with nothing more planned than a simple question to the group – "What sort of book shall we write?" we have every time managed to produce strong characters, interesting plots, good development and structure and where we have had the time, a complete novel.

Let me stress emphatically that there is no one way to write a book. Every writer has his/her own approach. Some need to retreat from the world and not emerge until a complete manuscript accompanies them. Others go to writing classes to get peer review and learn the techniques from other class members and the instructor. Some get writer's block, others never experience it. Some write fluently and easily, others grind it out.

The statistics of intended writers are startling and depressing; some 80% of all the developed countries' populations believe they have a book inside of them. About 4% of them will one day sit down and start work. 90% of those will not complete the first chapter as they realise how incredibly difficult it is to develop characters, plot lines, dialogue and continuity and how near-impossible it is to complete a full novel structured well enough to be read. Only about one tenth of one percent will get to write those magic words, *"The End."*

Then it gets harder as they try to get published.

I am quite certain that this book will help writers improve their chances quite well.

But while this book will greatly assist you in writing a novel, it will not help you write a *good* novel necessarily. It will not teach creative writing nor give you a wild imagination. For that, you will need to go elsewhere. Nor will it provide the courage to face the sheer hard, grinding work involved in creating a novel of perhaps 100,000 words or more, the polishing and reworking that can take ten times the amount of work involved in initially writing the book. It won't necessarily let you face the fear of letting friends and family read it for the first time, an experience that I liken to running naked down the High Street at rush hour. But this book *will* make all those steps easier as you find that you have accomplished the near-impossible feat of actually completing a book, it *will* make the mechanics easier and show you how to get started, how to structure your book, how to overcome the horrors of writer's block and how to think up plots, story lines and characters.

So, let's get started.

Chapter 1 – Getting Started

This may be the hardest part. Actually getting to the point where you have switched off the television, switched on the computer, taken pen in hand, picked up the recorder or whatever process you use, put the kids to bed, kicked the cat out, persuaded the spouse that you really, *really* want to do this, it now becomes clear that deciding to write a book is insane. Seriously, it's a fiendishly difficult thing to accomplish. So unless you already have a great idea and have thought about it long enough that the opening paragraph is in your head ready to be released, you are now facing the blank sheet or screen and this is terrifying.

So don't do it. Try another approach.

But a word of explanation; what I have done here is take a case-study of one workshop that I have run and used that to show the development of plot lines and characters, so there is a lot of detail in the examples to emphasise just what can be developed with the group synergy.

The probability is quite high that if you have reached this stage, you already know in which genre you are going to be writing. Is it the Family History? If so, that's another matter entirely and many writers' clubs and educational establishments offer courses specifically tailored to such a work as there is a growing demand for these books purely for family consumption. Is it a thriller? A romance? An historical drama? An adventure story? Crime drama? Science Fiction? All of the above? Here's a thought –

it may not matter. Don't be too committed to one genre. Many a writer has begun writing a book to find it becomes something quite different from what he or she intended at the start. *"Mickie Dalton"* began for me as a cathartic autobiography and stayed that way for five chapters before I realised the opening chapter had great potential to be the kids' sci-fi adventure I had always intended to write. I scrapped all but the first chapter and began again.

But with your decision now made to start this process, it is the time to adopt the Business School approach to solving problems and creating operational solutions and form your Work Group.

Who you invite into the group will make a big difference. My suggestion would be to start with three or four friends, maybe a relative, maybe your spouse, even perhaps one or more of your children. The key is to have people who understand and support your goal of writing a book that will be good enough to publish and sell to people who do not know you. Fellow writers from your Writers' Association would be a good population from which to select your group.

So think about whom you want, who you believe will support you and who can give the time you need. I believe that initially you really need only one session a week, perhaps no more than sixty to ninety minutes at a time for the first five or six weeks and you should advise the group members of this planned commitment. Unless you find yourself in one of those magical creative periods when the story flows like hot butter, plot lines write themselves and characters of astonishing complexity, brilliant backgrounds and charismatic personalities leap onto the whiteboard, an hour is about right. More than ninety minutes and fatigue can set in, causing stresses within the group. Anyway, the rest of your available time should be spent actually writing. Later in the process, you will need the group again.

The rules of engagement once the group has formed are quite simple:

1 – there are no bad ideas;

2 – it's not a competition in which the rights to an idea are claimed; an eventual brilliant idea that is adopted into the story is merely the end result of all of the group thinking and talking. It may have come initially from an idea that was eventually rejected, but had itself stimulated an idea in somebody else;

3 – no idea is too way-out to be considered;

4 – there must be no put-downs; see point 2;

5 – no combat. Don't fight to retain or throw out an idea – if the group is rejecting it, so be it, it wouldn't have worked anyway;

6 – get it all up on the whiteboard; and

7 – it is the author's responsibility to note down the contents of the board before it gets wiped.

And so you're ready for your book to start its gestation. If you want to lead the group, stand by the whiteboard. If one of the group is a skilled facilitator and discussion leader, he or she may be better suited, if willing, to lead the process.

Some time should be spent here on the role of the facilitator, because this can make or break the entire process. A good facilitator can generate magic, a poor one can let the group fall into confused, uncontrolled arguments that generate nothing but irritation and abandonment of the project.

The debating room must be a very safe place. There must never be any scoffing at an idea or suggestion, nor any rejection of an idea with contempt. While ideas will be rejected, it must be done for reasons that are clear and obvious and not in a negative manner.

The facilitator must control the group with a firm enough hand to ensure everybody gets heard and the group doesn't devolve into uncontrolled chaos, yet relaxed enough so that somebody else can go to the board if necessary and explore an idea.

The critical requirement is to ask the right questions and follow each thread until it seems exhausted, and move to another one as needed.

The questions are usually obvious, but sometimes the facilitator may see an opening that is not so obvious, perhaps because it aligns with the writer's existing ideas and themes, and follow that one through.

Like any classroom teacher, you must make sure that somebody is heard if they have something to say.

If the group is small enough and disciplined enough because of the members' maturity, it works easily as everybody will tend to be courteous enough to let others speak and know when to enter the conversation. If not, you should establish ground rules beforehand about when to speak, perhaps reverting to the classroom convention of simply raising a hand.

Make sure everybody is heard though, and don't make somebody wait so long to speak that they get fed up. You might lose a golden suggestion.

With adults, this is rarely a problem. So the biggest single requirement is to ensure the questions are asked and suggestions noted on the board.

One of the most common questions I get is "How do you think of a plot?" For the beginning writer, this can be a hurdle. For me now, I can find twenty story lines a day. It can be anything; a passing comment overheard in a crowd; an anecdote about a small event that leaves a "why?" or "how?" hanging in the air; a newspaper item; a weird car you saw on the road; just about anything.

So if you haven't yet worked out a basic story line, start now by listing anything that comes to mind and chatting with the group about the concept. For example:

The basic story-line of *"The Julie Malloy Gang and the Secret Agent"* which was written as a project with ten children at Rolland Plains Upper Primary School came from a story told to me by a friend who used to run a coat-checking business in Canada. He told me that somebody got the wrong case on checking out and later returned it for his own, but the owner of the returned case never came to claim it. The idea of "why" intrigued me for years, so I turned the kids onto it. I'm quite certain that the truth bears no resemblance to our story.

The premise of my sci-fi adventure *"The Humanity File"* (still under development – a working title only) came on hearing a speaker on television commenting that the vast majority of DNA seems to be junk. The idea jarred me, because Nature doesn't seem to be that wasteful. There's probably something else going on in those DNA strands. I went to my whiteboard and a couple of hours later had a story line that will get me shot by the religious right, but as I already have one book published with that capability, I'm not concerned.

I once heard a man in a crowded train in Sydney tell his friend how he'd been driving on a country road and some fool had nearly run him off the road. "Almost as if he'd wanted to," said the man.

Whoops. What if he *had* been trying to do just that? Why? What events had led up to that attempted murder? Could the intended victim even know just why somebody wanted him silenced? And all that led to my first and still unpublished novel, *"Corrupting Influences."* Such a scene didn't in fact eventuate in the book, but thinking about it resulted in a far more complex scenario.

So get a bit "loosey-goosy." Start noting ideas on the board, follow through with them, invite further suggestions. Ask members of the group to cite odd incidents or conversations. Let's imagine that the scenario of being run off the road was considered a possible trigger for a story. Now we get into the brainstorming. That scenario has possibilities.

First question: why did the unknown assailant try it? Does the victim have something or know something without being aware of what, that the assailant wants silenced or lost? Was it simple revenge? For what? Who is the intended victim?

As these questions are being asked, the facilitator must draw them out on the board. Each possible answer will result in more questions and immediately take you down paths you had never considered when the session started.

So in the early stages, we might have this up on the whiteboard (see Diagram 1):

So all of a sudden, you have the basic premise, an event which needs cause and effect, a puzzle and just as important, you have two characters, one of whom may remain unidentified until it suits you to reveal it. If you examine the diagram, you will almost certainly see more questions to be asked, more alternative answers and several branches along which a story could evolve. Even as I drew up this whiteboard on my own, I got new ideas and possibilities. A little one at the bottom, the reference to alien viruses, even opened up the possibility that this mystery-thriller could actually be a sci-fi adventure.

So now I would leave that small structure in place and go to another point of development, the main characters. We will come back to the plot.

But just think – you have started writing a novel. You haven't started where most people start, at the beginning. Actually, you have no idea where the story is. But you have made a start and it gets easier from here on.

BASIC PREMISE: YOU ARE DRIVING ALONG A COUNTRY ROAD &
ANOTHER CAR ATTEMPTS TO FORCE YOU OFF THE ROAD AT
A PARTICULARLY DANGEROUS SPOT

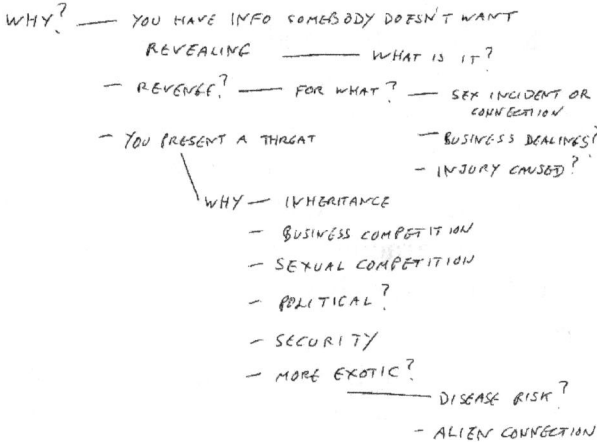

WHY? —— YOU HAVE INFO SOMEBODY DOESN'T WANT
        REVEALING ———— WHAT IS IT?
    — REVENGE? —— FOR WHAT? — SEX INCIDENT OR
                                   CONNECTION
  — YOU PRESENT A THREAT   — BUSINESS DEALINGS?
                       — INJURY CAUSED?
        WHY — INHERITANCE
           — BUSINESS COMPETITION
           — SEXUAL COMPETITION
           — POLITICAL?
           — SECURITY
           — MORE EXOTIC?
                   — DISEASE RISK?
               — ALIEN CONNECTION

WHO IS THE DRIVER

WHO IS THE CENTRAL CHARACTER?

Diagram 1 – The basic premise explored

Chapter 2 - Character Development

A book depends on its characters far more than on plot and story line. Granted that these are essential and no book will succeed without at least adequate story concepts, the fact is that a book can succeed and be intensely readable with a weak plot and strong characters, but the reverse is not true. Poorly defined and shallow characters with unrealistic, stilted dialogue will kill the best of plots and wildest of adventures.

So before you continue developing the story, get the characters developed. And as new characters enter the story – and you will probably have no idea who these might be as yet – perform this process of character development. In this process, you should go as far as you possibly can with each individual. Create backgrounds, histories, strengths, weaknesses, childhoods, educational standards, etc and go to the very end of the process. While the greatest part of the background you create may never appear in the story, what you will achieve is a three-dimensional individual who is as near to living and breathing as you can make him or her and as a result, his or her dialogue and reactions will dictate themselves to you until you experience the extraordinary sense of being merely the stenographer of a story happening in your head.

Every successful writer will have experienced this; it's what keeps us writing through the night sometimes because you dare not turn off the story being told for you to record.

So now try creating people.

Let's start with the central character in this story, the man who was almost killed by being run off the road. Get the group together and start asking the questions and recording the results to get the most complete personality drawn. Some of these qualities may be altered later as the story takes shape and perhaps veers off in quite unexpected directions as the brainstorming continues, but still you must develop your characters.

So: What is this man's name? His age? His profession? His appearance? Is he married? If so, is the marriage successful? Who and what is his wife? (And we must do a similar process for his wife.) What is his nationality, place of birth, ethnic beginning? Where was he brought up? What sort of education did he have? What sort of income? What are his hobbies, his interests, his reading preferences? What about his parents? His siblings, if any? His children, if any?

The process is a decision tree from which you can pick the path to develop your character, like this:

Premise – Man found dead at the wheel of a car at the bottom of the ravine

The man:
- Old (60+)
- Prime (30-60)
- Young (17-30)

Status
- Wealthy
- Middle Class
- Working Class

Education
- High School or below
- Bachelor Degree
- Graduate Degree (Masters/Doctorate)

Profession
- Executive
- Academic
- Management
- Manual/Clerical

Family
- Married → Happy / Unhappy
- Divorced
- Single
- Partner

Ethnic Origin
- Australian
- European/American
- Asian
- Indigenous
- Other

Hobbies/Activities
- Gambling
- Sports
- Collecting
- Creative arts
- Secret Vices

Family (children)
- None
- One or more
- Children
- Teenage
- Adult
- From previous marriage(s)

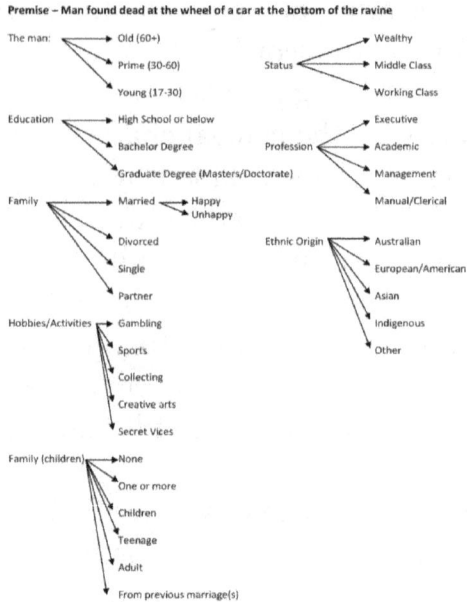

I can pretty well guarantee that the group will come alive during this exercise. I am invariably astonished by the imagination that is displayed when a group starts to create a person. Even when I did this exercise with a group of Primary School children, the results were fascinating. There is nothing like being a God-like entity and engaging in the act of Creation. In another exercise we will look at writing science fiction where this act of Creation goes to an even higher level and we can create an entire alien civilisation.

At the end of an hour, you might end up with something like this – see Diagram 2. This is just the beginning; we haven't yet explored his family relationships, his kids, certainly not his occupation all that much. And the process was a little different from the first exercise. When developing persons, the group tends to discuss each element of the individual and sometimes the result is coloured by the role the character is going to play. When developing Jens Petersen, the group started out knowing he was the central character and had to be capable of playing a role in some sort of mystery-thriller. So he was never going to be old, frail, stupid, illiterate, etc. But the facilitator must create an atmosphere which encourages the discussion and the synergy that leads to energetic discussion.

In reality, the process could easily have taken a full hour or two and filled up two whiteboards with all the extra details that will help flesh out the main protagonist. You would want to know exactly what his job is, what external interests he has, such as hobbies, possible marital infidelities, his relationship with his children, etc

But let me point again how powerful this process is; as I started it on my own, one question was where was this man born? I don't know why his nationality was Swedish, it just happened that way. Rather than simply picking the Swedish Capital, Stockholm for his place of birth, I went to the atlas, looked at a map of the country and saw Uppsala, which I knew was a famous University town. That opened up some possibilities that hadn't been there before. If perhaps we decided that Jens Petersen would be an academic or scientist engaged in some scientific venture, that just could be a part of why somebody wants him dead. It may not happen that way, but a new possible branch was created. That's why I created him as a chemist, with a Masters' degree.

MAIN CHARACTER

JENS PETERSEN b 1968, UPPSALA, SWEDEN
PARENTS— KARL & LOTTE, BOTH ACADEMICS AT UPPSALA
KARL A PHYSICIST, MOTHER A BIOLOGIST
EMIGRATED TO AUSTRALIA 1972, PARENTS TAUGHT AT
U. OF NSW. JENS WENT TO PRIMARY SCHOOL &
HS IN EASTERN SUBURBS — VERY BRIGHT IN SCIENCES,
AVERAGE IN ARTS, BUT LOVED GREEK/ROMAN/NORSE
MYTHOLOGY
NOT VERY SCANDINAVIAN LOOKS — MID HEIGHT, TENDS TO
OVERWEIGHT, PLAYED SOCCER & CRICKET OK, NOT A
SURFIE, SO SOME LIMITS ON SOCIAL/SEX LIFE! GOOD AT
CHESS, QUITE SELF CONFIDENT
GRADUATED + HONOURS AT SYDNEY U. IN CHEMISTRY, THEN
MSC. NOW HIS HAIR IS THINNING, GETTING HEAVIER,
LOVES JAPANESE & INDIAN CUISINE, THEN EUROPEAN.
NOT MUCH OF A READER ANYMORE.
DRIVES A COMMODORE, RED, COMPETANT DRIVER. WORKS
FOR AN ENGINEERING FIRM IN SOUTHERN SUBURBS.
NOT A GREAT TRAVELLER — TO USA TWICE ON BUSINESS
ONCE TO EUROPE AFTER GRADUATION — TOURED SWEDEN,
TOOK IN ART MUSEUMS IN HOLLAND & MET SUZANNE.
EARNS $105,000 pa, HAS AVERAGE 3-BED HOUSE IN
CLOVELLY

Diagram 2 – Initial character creation

Sometimes, the writer does not use the group brainstorming approach for this stage, at least not for the central character(s) as he or she has a colourful imagination and/or sets out to describe somebody already known.

However, I recommend using the group because the results can be amazing and will almost always result in a more complex protagonist than had been originally considered. And even if you choose to work alone, still use the whiteboard, stand up there in pro-active mode, draw out the character, let him or her start to take shape in your mind. I can do this alone and still surprise myself with the complexity of who I create.

For example, on my own, this is what I came up with for the initial design of two of the characters in my developing sci-fi work, *"The Humanity File."*

Karen Petrova

Born in Kiev, 1942, only daughter of Karl Petrov, chemist, Nobel Prize winner in 1962 for chemical synthesis of artificial skin used for wound and burn treatment; and Ekaterina, daughter of a communist party official, member of the Soviet Politburo in 1935-1940. The family had been able to leave Russia in 1964 for the UK during Kruschev's Thaw. Karen had completed two years of degree in pharmacology at Leningrad University, was able to complete First Class Honours degree at Birmingham, then PhD (1970), then Post Doctoral at M.I.T., 1971-1972.

Lecturer at London U. 1973 - 1975

Married Hector Forbes of Edinburgh, a pharmacist, in 1975. The Forbes family was wealthy, Forbes was a research pharmacologist with a generic pharmacological company in London, but set up a private research laboratory after the marriage so that they could follow up some ideas and earlier work of Forbes'. They developed a compound that stabilised cholesterol and blood pressure and patented it, formed the company Life Technology in 1980 after two years of clinical trials and government approval. Hugely successful, enormously wealthy, they licensed the product to a major firm and devoted Life Technology to further research and set up a spin-off, "Blueprint" to research DNA, a long-time fascination of both of them. Hector died in 1990, she now devotes her time to running a few foundations with some hands-on time at Blueprints. They had no children.

She is now 66, 170cm tall, very slender and fit, runs 10k every morning, has a 50 acre estate in Berkshire and an apartment behind Harrods in London. Paints water-colours, has had one exhibition in 1993, but lacks true artistic passion. Still speaks with a Russian accent and some idiom, but friends and colleagues suspect she has a perfect command of English and the accent is a small idiosyncrasy. She dresses in very expensive style, flowing dresses, drives a yellow Maserati, but not very well.

The plant is in the industrial estate on the Thames Valley Park, east of Reading.

William "Bill" Hawker

Born 1978 in Leeds, Leeds GS, Leeds U at 17, having completed GS two years ahead of time. Considered to have genius level IQ, offered several scholarships including

Cambridge, First Class Honours B.Sc in Biology, 1998, straight to Doctorate in Genetics, graduated in 2001. Father (Gerry) ran a tobacconist, Mother (Jennifer) was a history teacher at a secondary school.

Bill is 188cm, heavy build, broad face, lots of hair but clean-shaven, looks like a farm-boy, confused expression sometimes taken for slowness, but is in fact frustration that everybody else is so slow. He's unmarried, few relationships as he scares off women. Reads Sci-fi, loves to exchange ideas of futurism with Garry. With that 180+ IQ, he has picked up seriously advanced electronic instrumentation skills. Has a huge collection of old British comedy programs, Goon Show, Round the Horn, Hancock, Goodies, Monty Python, etc.

On collecting his doctorate, was swamped with Post-Doc and lectureship positions in UK and USA, decided to travel for a year before making a decision. While in Sydney, he heard about the creation of Blueprints, called up Life Technology, pleaded his case and was hired on the spot.

But as I further developed the novel, new events, unforeseen complications, turns and twists that I had never anticipated made some changes essential to the main characters. But this is natural, absolutely bound to happen and is in fact a sign of
the creativity muse at work. However, even in this small development I went to the internet, confirmed that there still is a Leeds Grammar School where Bill Hawker was a student, that the University of

Birmingham offered the right programs, found a map of Reading and located the industrial park by the Thames where once were just fields when I used to row there as a schoolboy, and so on.   See the discussion later about researching your facts.

I haven't used all these characteristics in describing these characters, but I did start off with living, breathing characters to make the book readable and largely write itself.

Let's get back to essential characters;   how about Jens' wife?   For this, I will go to an exercise I ran with a group of seniors and this is similar to what we came up with.   See diagram 3.   In fact, we came up with a lot more than this, but I've shortened the page for clarity.   But as I developed this, some more ideas came for Jens' character.   I'd forgotten if he spoke with any accent, so now we can update his description with a slight European accent that confuses people somewhat.

But always be prepared to go back and modify your characters' descriptions if something develops that requires a different characteristic.

Having got two key protagonists, we should continue to develop them further;   continue the exercise with their whole background;   how did they meet?   Was one of them travelling in the other's country, or both of them somewhere else, say at an art museum in Holland?

How did the families respond?   Supportive? Hostile?   My group was pretty sure that Suzanne's

Quebecois family would be wildly hostile, and this was the prompt that sent them to live in Australia.

Then, assuming that Jens is the central protagonist, we should go back and further expand his profile.

SUZANNE PELLETIER, b 1970 QUEBEC CITY TO
ALAIN & ANNA-MARIE PELLETIER, OLD LANDED GENTRY
ORIGINAL FAMILIES IN QUEBEC — V. RICH, V. RIGHT WING
EDUCATION — U. OF MONTREAL REJECTS, REBELLED AGAINST
    FAMILY, WENT TO ENGLISH-SPEAKING McGILL U. IN
    MONTREAL — STUDIED CLASSICAL ART.
SPORTS? — HIGHLY KLUTZY, USELESS AT EVERYTHING
READS — NOT A LOT, MOSTLY ROMANCE & HISTORICAL
DISTANT FROM PARENTS — LIVED IN ENGLISH AREA OF
    MONTREAL UNTIL SHE MARRIED JENS
SHE IS MEDIUM HEIGHT — 168 CMS, ONCE SLIM,
    STARTING TO EXPAND.
SPEAKS WITH NO OBVIOUS FRENCH ACCENT.
WORKED AT AN ART STUDIO IN MONTREAL UNTIL
GOING TO AUSTRALIA TO JOIN JENS, NOW RUNS
A FAIRLY SUCCESSFUL STUDIO ON QUEEN ST.
IN WOOLLAHA, SYDNEY
DRIVES MERCEDES SUV, TAKES YOUNGEST DAUGHTER (6)
& COLLECTS FROM SNOTTY-NOSED PRIVATE SCHOOL
IN VAUCLUSE
ELDER DAUGHTER IS 14, GOING ON 24.

Diagram 3 – Suzanne Pelletier

This is just the start. I cannot emphasise enough that the process requires the biggest amount of effort and should be as complete as possible so that the characters come alive and their dialogue will be realistic, as will their reactions to events. As long as your group continues to have ideas and the enthusiasm to keep creating, keep playing God.

But a word of warning. Be careful not to create an existing living or fictional character without realising it. Unconsciously creating an evil protagonist who is a direct copy of somebody you detest can cause you problems. If your character development is going too smoothly, especially if doing it alone, or you are directing your group down a path that seems too easy, you may well be falling into a trap. I nearly went there when creating a sci-fi villain who was developing wonderfully and it bothered me until I realised I was describing an entity from a sci-fi comic *"Eagle"* from my childhood.

Immediate changes were implemented.

Chapter 3 – Back to the Plot Development

So at this point, you can go back to the plot line and start to explore possibilities. Start with one of the options that came up when developing the basic premise of a plot, the possibility of some form of disease being involved. There's no special reason why one would pick one over another, but this is a reasonable example. Perhaps one of the group members is a medical person or a chemist and notes that we have given Jens a professional qualification of an M.Sc. in Chemistry. You may want to expand on that, and define Organic, Physical or Inorganic Chemistry, but the group may not want to develop to that extent, depending on membership. Though at a later stage, you may need to be more precise if the story line develops to a stage where it's critical. So, having plumped for a disease as being a major factor in why somebody is trying to kill Jens, go back to the board and start following the paths that get identified. After 30-60 minutes of spirited debate, this could be the answer see (Diagram 4).

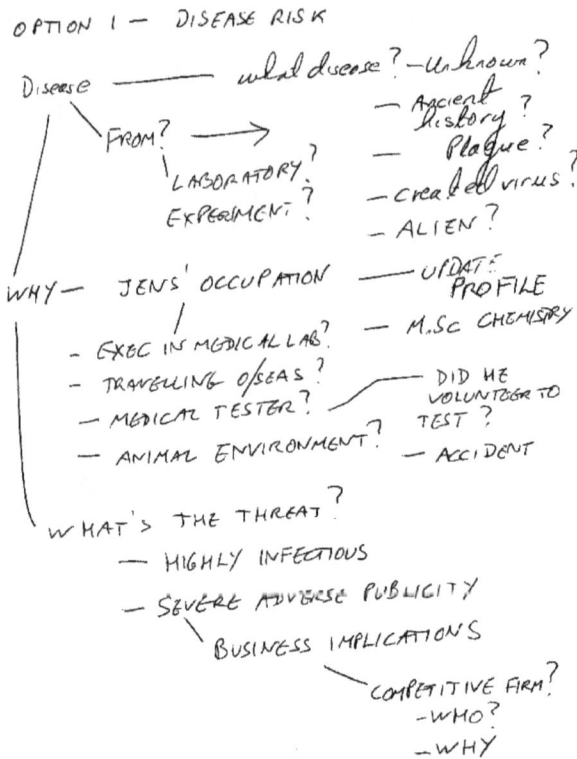

OPTION 1 — DISEASE RISK

Disease ———— what disease? — unknown?

— Ancient History?
FROM? ——>
— Plague?
LABORATORY? — created virus!
EXPERIMENT. — ALIEN?

WHY — JENS' OCCUPATION ——— UPDATE PROFILE
— M.Sc CHEMISTRY
- EXEC IN MEDICAL LAB?
- TRAVELLING O/SEAS? ——— DID HE VOLUNTEER TO TEST?
— MEDICAL TESTER?
— ANIMAL ENVIRONMENT. — ACCIDENT

WHAT'S THE THREAT?
—— HIGHLY INFECTIOUS
— SEVERE ADVERSE PUBLICITY
BUSINESS IMPLICATIONS
COMPETITIVE FIRM?
— WHO?
— WHY

Diagram 4 – Disease Risk Option

There are several obvious paths that could be taken, just from this one small branch of the initial development. It can be business espionage, medical thriller with some exotic disease running out of control, international espionage involving biological warfare, even sci-fi again, with perhaps a created virus being lost, an alien virus (bringing us into Michael Crichton territory), an ancient pre-historical plague reappearing, and so on. There are about three distinct thriller plots just from this section. And there are still paths to explore, each with many branches. For example, who or what will be damaged or otherwise hurt if the plot involves competitive corporations or individuals, or even governments?

At this stage, depending on the path(s) chosen by the group, quite a lot of research will be identified as essential. This topic will be covered in a later stage, but one ESSENTIAL rule should be laid out here, one that can make or break a novel if ignored, depending on the reader. The rule is:

GET YOUR FACTS CORRECT.

One of the finest writers of the modern day, as far as I'm concerned, and one who influenced me greatly in my initial development, is Dick Francis. No, he's not a candidate for a Pulitzer, his works are probably not studied in English Literature curricula at schools or Universities, but Francis worked very hard on his research and he got his facts straight. While all his stories involved horses in one way or another, hardly surprising, given his background as a top-class jockey, whether writing about photography, medicine, flying or anything else, he did the research and made sure the basis of his stories was rock solid.

We'll expand on this a little later.

Let's try another story line branch; Jens has information that must be suppressed. This again opens up innumerable opportunities and I can see about five distinct plots revealed here alone.

The results after perhaps an hour of what is normally highly entertaining debate and brainstorming could well look like Diagram 5.

Is the dangerous information political, corporate, scientific or personal? What is the nature of the information in each of those categories and others, if the group identifies more? Did Jens get the information by accident? Was it placed on him, if so by whom and why? Did he steal it? If so, this opens up more complex issues about our lead protagonist, such as why did he do it? What is the motivation and potential pay-off?

Good or bad reasons? If the information is revealed, what would be the political, corporate or personal results?

The group will probably follow all these paths, or because of personal and/or professional interest, tend to focus on specific branches. That's perfectly okay, the writer is after all just looking for one story, but even this early in the process, several individual story lines have been identified which could be incorporated into political, action or crime thriller, science fiction, even a romantic thriller.

OPTION — INFORMATION TO BE SUPPRESSED

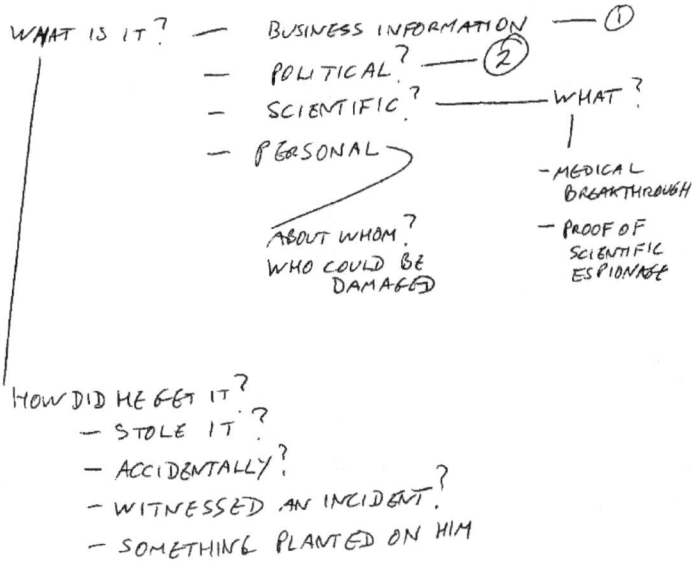

WHAT IS IT? — BUSINESS INFORMATION — ①
     — POLITICAL? — ②
     — SCIENTIFIC? — WHAT?
     — PERSONAL

        — MEDICAL BREAKTHROUGH

ABOUT WHOM?
WHO COULD BE DAMAGED

     — PROOF OF SCIENTIFIC ESPIONAGE

HOW DID HE GET IT?
     — STOLE IT?
     — ACCIDENTALLY?
     — WITNESSED AN INCIDENT?
     — SOMETHING PLANTED ON HIM

① — COMPETITIVE INFORMATION?
     CORPORATE SECRETS?
     ILLEGAL ACTIVITIES
       OR CONNECTIONS
          — WHAT WOULD HAPPEN IF REVEALED?

② — DAMAGING REVELATIONS?
     — BUDGET SECRETS?
     — BEHAVIOUR/RELATIONSHIPS
     — CORPORATE DEALINGS
     — INTERNATIONAL CONNECTIONS

Diagram 5 – The suppressed information option

If I were writing this book and conducting these brainstorming sessions, I would have seen some further opportunities for complex plot lines, and I would now take the conversation to a further development of the backgrounds of Jens and Suzanne and both their families.

Start with Suzanne's French Canadian ancestry, something close to my heart because of the years I spent living in Canada, especially Montreal.

Depending on the personal knowledge of the group's members, the brainstorming could take many paths and result in different levels of complexity. But the first stage could result in something like Diagram 6. Now the reason the Pelletier family profile is not exactly that of a warm, loving family is because the thought that came to mind as I developed this story line for this book, was that perhaps the bad guys in the story who want Jens dead could actually be Suzanne's family.

SUZANNE'S PARENTS

FATHER - ALAIN, b 1941 IN QUEBEC CITY FROM MANY
GENERATIONS OF PELLETIERS, BACK TO BEFORE
CANADIAN FEDERATION IN 1867, BANKING & RURAL
HOLDINGS, V. WEALTHY & V. RIGHT WING. FAMILY
HAD BEEN VICHY SYMPATHISERS IN WWII. DID
ACCOUNTING & FINANCE AT MONTREAL U., RUNS SEVERAL
INVESTMENT COMPANIES, SPEAKS FR. ALWAYS, RARELY
ENGLISH, RARELY TRAVELS OUTSIDE THE PROVINCE.
STRONGLY SUPPORTS QUÉBEC SEPARATION, SHORT
OVERWEIGHT, SMOKES CIGARS, DRIVES A CADILLAC

ANNA-MARIE, NÉE LEMOINE, b 1945 IN
TROIS RIVIÈRES TO MINOR BUT WEALTHY POLITICAL
FAMILY, ALSO ~~WEALTHY &~~ V. RIGHT WING. SHE
DID ART & FRENCH LITERATURE AT QUEBEC U.,
NEVER WORKED AT ANY JOB. DILITENTE
ARTIST OF MEDIOCRE LANDSCAPES. SECRET
BUT SEVERE ALCOHOLIC, DRINKS VODKA.
SPEAKS GOOD BUT ACCENTED ENGLISH, ALSO
STRONG SEPARATIST.
THEY HAD A SON BEFORE SUZANNE, HE
DIED OF LEUKEMIA AT 13 MONTHS OLD

Diagram 6 – Suzanne's Parents

This could be a good fit for many of the branches that have been developed so far, and this option will show in one of the whiteboard layouts to come. So while almost everybody I knew and still know in Montreal and in the Province of Quebec are charming, intelligent people, I certainly did meet a few who could fit the profile I have created here and I need some "baddies" for the story.

So already, we have developed several story lines. In fact there are many – tracking along each of the branches so far laid out would provide an individual story line. Let's look at some of the possibilities that we have already identified, with a little more imagination applied as we follow some of those paths.

Remember the first plot options we developed? Go back to Diagram 4 and we had this section developed:

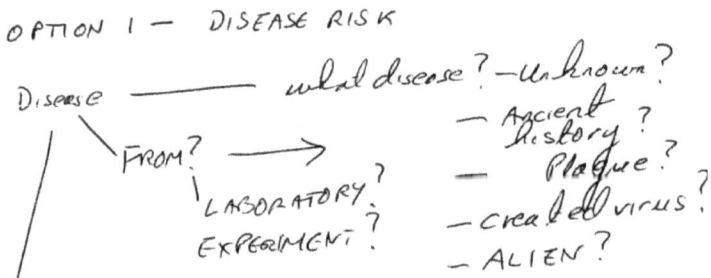

OPTION 1 — DISEASE RISK

Disease ———— what disease? — Unknown?
— Ancient History?
— Plague?
FROM? ———>
— created virus?
LABORATORY?
EXPERIMENT? — ALIEN?

Suppose we had taken that path that gave us a created virus and played further with it, asking the questions and documenting the suggestions that gave us this new path:

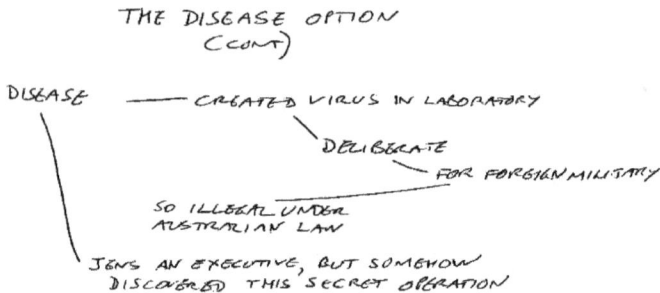

THE DISEASE OPTION
(cont)

DISEASE ———— CREATED VIRUS IN LABORATORY
DELIBERATE
— FOR FOREIGN MILITARY
SO ILLEGAL UNDER AUSTRALIAN LAW
JENS AN EXECUTIVE, BUT SOMEHOW DISCOVERED THIS SECRET OPERATION

So here now is a complete initial plot:

Story 1 – Jens is a senior executive in a medical research establishment who has learned about a secret experiment that has developed a virus that could be used for biological warfare by a foreign country. This is a criminal, possibly treasonous venture. The company's ownership has realised Jens has learned of the development and cannot let him reveal the fact.

Let's play this game with some other strands. If we refer back to Diagram 5, the suppressed information option, there was a branch that suggested business information was the subject, and this led to another range of possibilities, thus:

After further brainstorming with your group, you might end up with this set of possibilities.

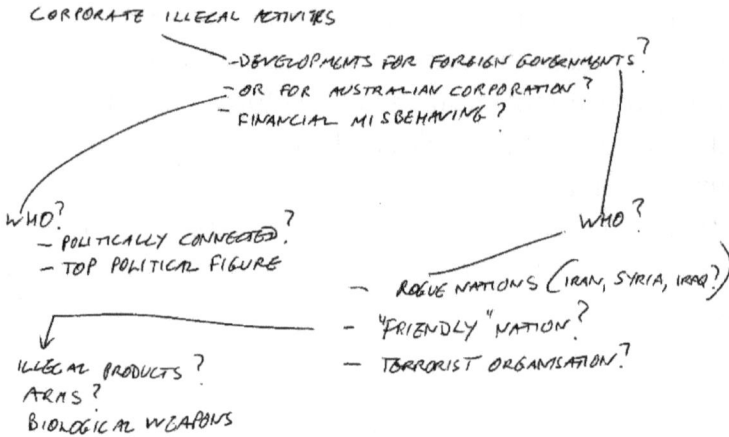

There are some similarities with the previous options concerning a virus development, and you may then decide to combine the story lines. But there are also some possibilities that lead you down paths of international espionage and/or some nasty political involvements at home. Depending on your personal preferences and literary tastes, you have now found some story lines to be developed further.

Here's the second optional story line, taken from following one of the paths in the above chart:

Jens discovers that his corporation has been developing products (not yet identified) for a foreign government with the illicit support of a senior government individual or politician and the revelation could destroy that individual, the company and potentially bring down the government while also generating massive anger throughout the world directed at the foreign country. That country could be one of the conventional villains, such as Iran or Iraq, but you might decide to follow a story line that makes a so-called "friendly" nation the culprit.

All this from a passing comment by a man that I overheard on a train.

And we haven't even looked yet at who is really behind the criminal acts, other than Jen's company. That opens up another whole field for imaginative brainstorming. Let's have a look at a few ideas as they develop on the whiteboard (Diagram 7).

Now almost certainly, my preference would be to follow the path of Suzanne's family being behind this whole plot. Just look at the possibilities that this opens up. There could be enormous hidden family secrets, Suzanne can be developed into either an evil, treasonous bitch or a victimised daughter escaping her dreadful family and discovering what they are really up to. So lots of opportunity for the interpersonal stuff to develop.

Or you could follow down the domestic political implications and look at possible treason within the government of the day or by certain agencies. In fact, you could combine just about that whole diagram into a wonderfully complex tale of international intrigue.

So you can almost certainly see how the power of a group has identified and developed several themes that you might never have seen had you sat in front of that awful empty page or computer screen and tried to think of a thriller story line alone.

WHO IS BEHIND IT?

FOREIGN GROUP?
- ISLAMIC?
- NEO-NAZI?
- OTHER TERRORIST?

FINANCED BY?
- USUAL SUSPECTS?
  - IRAN
  - SAUDI
  etc
- FOREIGN GOVT?
- PRIVATE CAPITALISTS?

FOREIGN NATION?
- WHO?

USUAL SUSPECTS?
- IRAN
- IRAQ
- SAUDI ARABIA

OTHER?
- EUROPEAN NATION!
- CHINA?
- JAPAN
- N/S AMERICAN?

DOMESTIC?
AUSTRALIAN GOVT?
AUST. PRIVATE?
POLITICAL GROUP?

SUZANNE'S FAMILY?
WHY?
SUPPORTING WHO?   DO THEY OWN JENS' COMPANY

DOES SUZANNE KNOW?
IS SHE PART OF IT? — YES? WHAT IMPLICATIONS
                          FOR FAMILY RELATION.
NO?   — THE CHILDREN?
WHAT IMPLICATIONS FOR   — WHO IS SHE, REALLY
THE FAMILY?

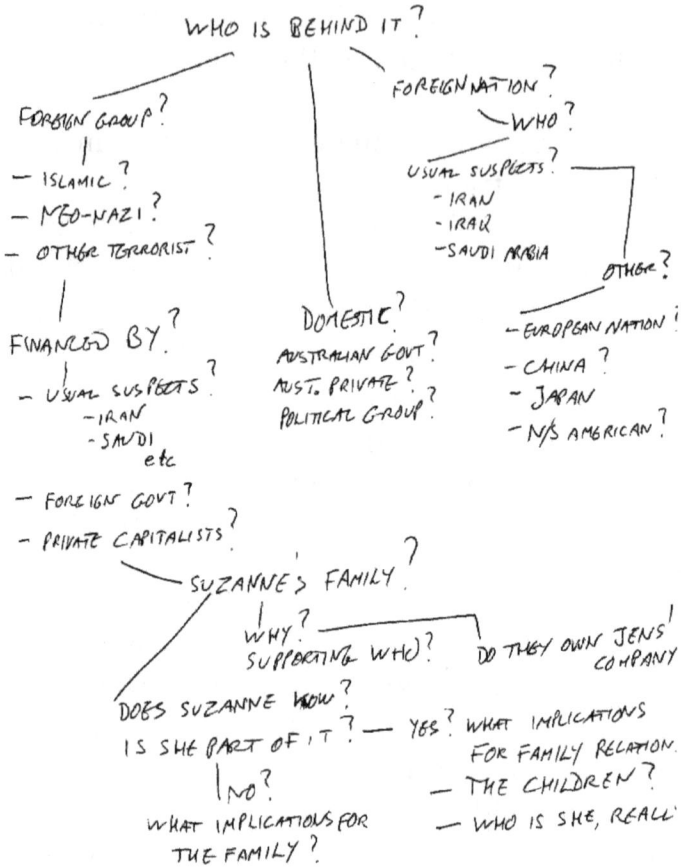

Diagram 7 – Who is behind this and why?

But do leave the story open to development. As your imagination grows (and you will be amazed at how much your capacity to dream up new situations or complexities develops as you do this stuff), new twists and turns will come to you. So don't try and plot out the entire book through to the conclusion, you will be limiting yourself. I know that there are many writers who know exactly how their books will develop, from the opening sequence to the final sentence. I'm not one of them and I find that ability incomprehensible. I have never begun a book with anything but a hazy idea of where it will go, and no book of mine yet has ended in anything vaguely resembling even that hazy idea.

If you're lucky, you will at some point have that "Holy $##*!!" moment when you see an opening for a wild swing in direction, a whole new possibility opening up, a complete new dimension to the story. It may not be you who sees it, but one of the group and it could be a simple blinding revelation or an off-the-cuff comment that suddenly brings the entire room to a dead silence.

A couple of times with my group of students doing the Mickie Dalton series, one young person made a casual suggestion that felt like an electric shock and I saw a marvellous sub-plot open up. I clearly remember when Sam Troutman casually suggested that one of the alien kids in the story would rediscover an ancient and lost capacity for telepathy within his species. I had to sit down, so great was the shock as I saw a whole new development reveal itself. But Sam had mentioned it quite casually and the rest of the class was already off on another topic and I could easily have lost it.

This does underline one of the key responsibilities of the group facilitator – you have to listen very carefully to everything and draw the group back to something if you feel it is critical.

Let's continue a little further and get into the development of the action. A likely place to start the book would be the attempted murder of Jens by the unknown driver of the other car. Starting with action or mystery is always a good approach.

For example, you could open the novel with a line such as,

"From nowhere at all, the Toyota Land Cruiser appeared in Jens Petersen's rear-view mirror and seemed to be sitting right on his tail."

You describe the fear, the sudden smash of the following car into Jens' rear end, the struggle to keep control and the blind terror as he is forced off the road, down a steep incline and the loss of consciousness as he crashes at the bottom. This can be followed by his recovery, the pain, the terrible climb back to the road and so on.

But then what? The group will now consider the following action and the facilitator plots the options on the board and lets the story develop. This could result in Diagram 8.

As you see, this session has identified a number of branches for the story. Does Jens know what he has got that is making somebody murderous? Has he deliberately stolen information? Why? What's the background to all this? That question now opens up an interesting possibility of a flash-back to many years before that could explain Jens' behaviour, motivations, all sorts of things.

Now you can see just what an incredible spider's web you can weave with this process. In just these few examples, the group could have identified a number of thriller story lines involving industrial espionage, possibly international and political drama, a deeply personal story of marital stress that itself could be part of the espionage themes, could end in tragedy for the family or could result happily in a stronger family unit. You could fill many pages with these diagrams and they should be filed away for later reference, review, further development, selection of an alternative story line or whatever is found to be useful.

AFTER CRASH

GETS BACK TO ROAD
PASSING MOTORIST HELP ?
USES MOBILE PHONE ?

POLICE & HOSPITAL
         —— DOES HE TELL THE FULL STORY ?

YES ?   NO ?
   MAYBE HE DOESN'T   WHY NOT ?
   KNOW WHAT'S GOING ON ?   — DOES HE KNOW
                                                          WHAT'S HAPPENING

   WHERE NEXT ?   — TOO TERRIFIED
   FURTHER EFFORTS TO KILL HIM ?   TO TALK

   WHEN WILL HE CATCH ON ?   — DOES HE KNOW
                                                      WHAT IS THE DATA
                                                      HE HAS ?

— IS HE INJURED ?   HOW BADLY
   — WIFE VISITS ?
                 —— IS HER BEHAVIOUR SUSPICIOUS ?
   — KIDS ?
   —COMPANY PEOPLE ? DOES JENS SUSPECT HER ?

   WHEN WILL HE GO BACK TO WORK

      — WHAT IS THEIR REACTION ?   WHAT REACTIONS ?
                                                          BACK AT WORK ?

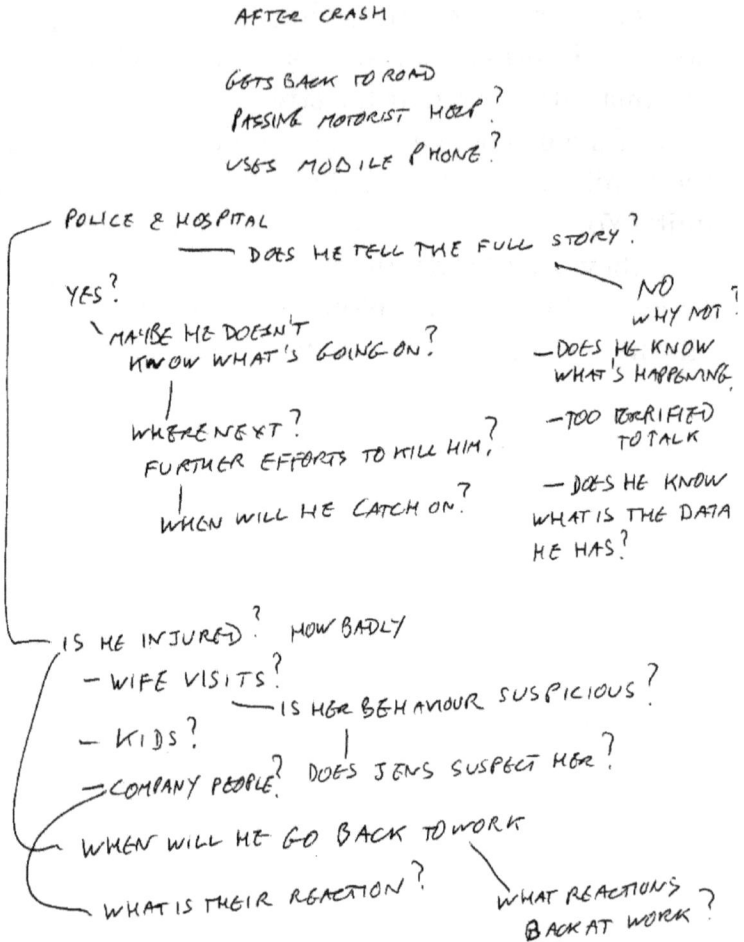

Diagram 8 – Immediately after the smash

In many ways, what the process does is create a sort of Universal Novel Generator!

A standard Business Decision Tree has been developed and you the writer can pick the branches you would like to follow. In the following example, the premise is that the driver went off the road, down a ravine and was killed.

This first stage, creating the outline of the victim was shown in an earlier chapter:

Then the second stage, deciding what the motive for murder could be:

The Motive(s)

Premise – Man found dead at the wheel of a car at the bottom of the ravine

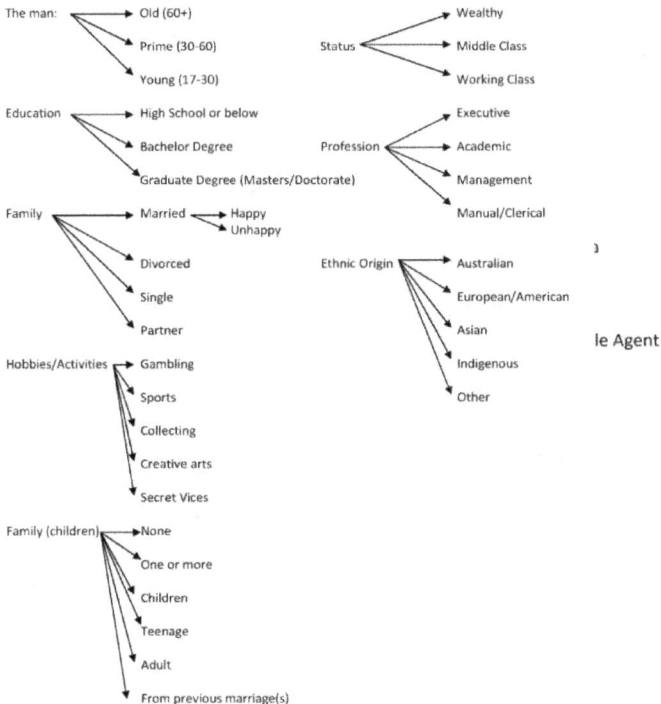

The man:	Old (60+)		Status	Wealthy
	Prime (30-60)			Middle Class
	Young (17-30)			Working Class

The man:
- Old (60+)
- Prime (30-60)
- Young (17-30)

Status:
- Wealthy
- Middle Class
- Working Class

Education:
- High School or below
- Bachelor Degree
- Graduate Degree (Masters/Doctorate)

Profession:
- Executive
- Academic
- Management
- Manual/Clerical

Family:
- Married → Happy / Unhappy
- Divorced
- Single
- Partner

Ethnic Origin:
- Australian
- European/American
- Asian
- Indigenous
- Other

le Agent

Hobbies/Activities:
- Gambling
- Sports
- Collecting
- Creative arts
- Secret Vices

Family (children):
- None
- One or more
- Children
- Teenage
- Adult
- From previous marriage(s)

Then this is followed by the discovery that what was thought to be an obvious accident is actually murder:

The Discovery that it's Murder

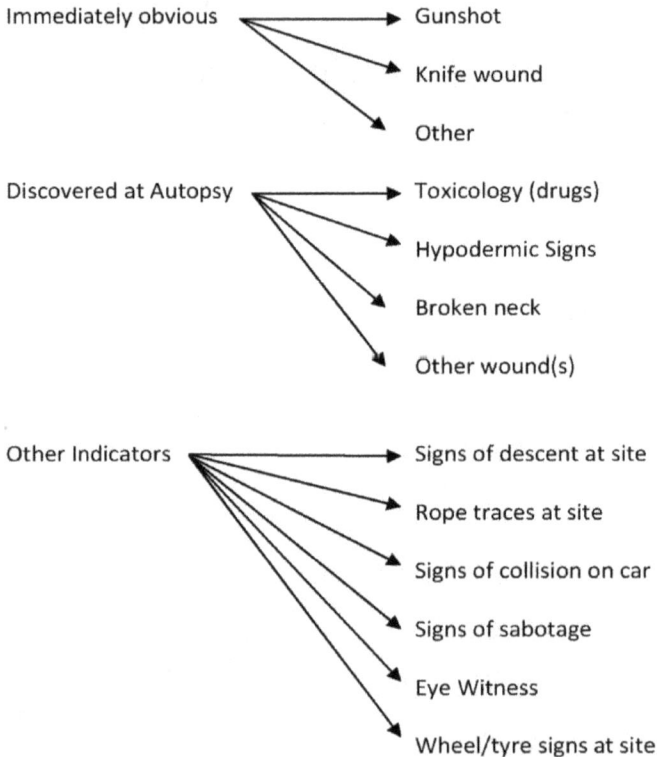

Immediately obvious → Gunshot
→ Knife wound
→ Other

Discovered at Autopsy → Toxicology (drugs)
→ Hypodermic Signs
→ Broken neck
→ Other wound(s)

Other Indicators → Signs of descent at site
→ Rope traces at site
→ Signs of collision on car
→ Signs of sabotage
→ Eye Witness
→ Wheel/tyre signs at site

Now you have a story line, you can flesh it out, add the details and continue the process until you have a book.

However, there are two further critical factors to be considered, that of focus and the personal development of the central character.

The Book's Focus

In business writing, it's sometimes called "The Payoff Concept." That great teacher of screenplay writing, John McKee calls it "The Controlling Factor." Whatever the term, whether business writing, screenplays or fiction of any genre, the rule is essential; the story should drive to a real, specific and achieved point. In romance novels, it's the culmination of all the crises, hurdles and difficulties the lovers face when they finally get together. In the detective novel, it's the successful conclusion to the battle of wits between detective and killer. In the "Quest" novel, the hero finally achieves the goal.

Regardless of back stories, romance threads within the thriller or any other thread, be clear on what the book's focus is and stay on course. The detective book should not veer off and become a romance or sci-fi story or anything but a battle of wits between killer and detective culminating in a win for the detective.

Pick the objective of the story and drive toward it. Everything else is colour and background.

Personal Development of the Character(s)

The story should be realistic in all ways, regardless of genre. The characters are human beings, not plastic dummies and human beings are affected by their experiences, whether for good or bad, depending on the writer.

So some change must occur within the central character as the story progresses if it is to be realistic. If not the central character, then somebody closely associated with that character. The change may not be as extreme as in my kids' sci-fi trilogy where Mickie Dalton grows from being a frightened, shy, abused 12-year old to perhaps the most powerful individual in the Universe as a 15-year old. Little obvious change occurs with Chief Inspector Morse during the series except for his increasing age, though he does become more grouchy, more cynical. More change occurs with his partner, Sergeant Lewis who grows in experience and ability and defers to his boss less and less through the series.

So the writer should give careful consideration to the main characters and develop them in a way that reflects the story and adds extra dimensions to it.

Chapter 4 - Secondary Story Lines

Some stories require that not all the book is directly related to the primary plot. There may be secondary plots, such as a developing romance or some associated crimes being committed, or simply some lifelines that can make fascinating reading. Arthur Hailey was the past master of the technique in his books such as *"Airport," "Hotel,"* and others, and I have used this approach as well in one of my still-developing books, *"Prescription for a Killing."* Used well, it can augment the book with some solidly human stories, but used badly, these stories just become padding. The secondary stories should relate to the primary plot in some way and if nothing else, do what the original character development did and significantly augment the three-dimensional nature of your characters.

Sometimes, developing the secondary story can generate a really useful idea for the primary plot and add dimensions and layers to it. And apart from that, it can be a lot of fun.

Let me give you an example from the book I mentioned above, *"Prescription for a Killing,"* a book I started some years ago about a company being attacked by religious fanatics because of its work in genetic modification. Initial attacks target the computer installation and one of the minor characters is the operations manager who will conduct the systems recovery at a "hot site" a few miles away. I started by describing how he had met a particularly sexy young lady in a bar and was in the middle of a steamy sexual relationship.

I also had the company's Human Resources manager, a young woman who had also embarked on a new relationship. I drew up the stories on the board and suddenly saw something useful.

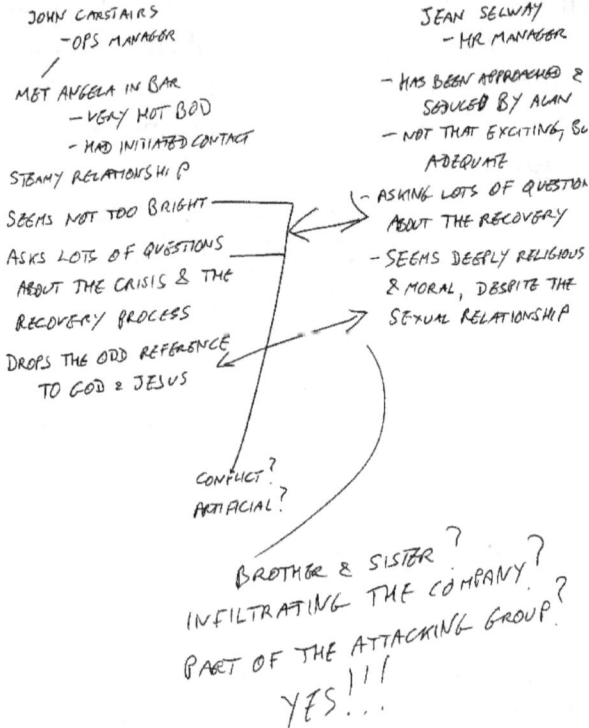

Diagram 9 – How secondary stories can work

Suddenly I had a whole sub-plot that fitted in nicely with the main story and also provided some opportunities for "human interest" elements to be included in the story.

If you do go this way, the risk is that you can overdo the human interest stuff and get maudlin or simply irrelevant. Developed well, however, it can add significant dimensions to the story and provide a great deal of extra depth to the characters. You may not get as good as Arthur Hailey, but then not many do. Mind you, while he did it wonderfully well, sometimes I got a bit irritated. I never could see what relevance to the plot there could be in *"Airport"* that some young lady had embarked on a major program of silicone injections to enlarge her breasts. Those monster boobs had nothing to do with the story that I could ever see.

Which should lead us to the subject of sex. My recommendation is - don't go overboard. There is no need for steamy sex scenes, graphic descriptions, etc. If the story calls for it to happen, just let it be implied, start the process but leave it there. It really doesn't move the story along. This subject will be explored further in a later chapter.

If you want to try pornography, do it in a separate genre. I try it now and again, but then I start laughing at the silliness.

See the earlier comments on the book's focus.

Chapter 5 – The Structure of a Book

One popular quote at Western's Business School was *"There's nothing so practical as a good theory."* Time and time again we proved this, by developing a theoretical structure by which to solve a problem and almost immediately seeing how to derive a solution.

The same approach works with developing a story. But there are several structures that can be used to form the book.

The Linear Story

This is the simplest structure. The story begins at the chronological beginning and continues in a straight development, usually from the point of view (pov) of a single character or perhaps a group of connected characters to the end. Examples of this structure are most children's books and books in the "Odyssey" format. An occasional variation is the flashback, used to explain a mystery or fill out a character's history.

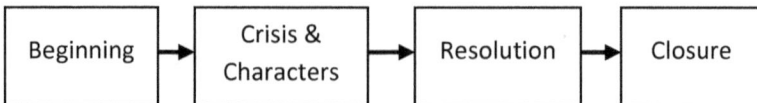

| Beginning | → | Crisis & Characters | → | Resolution | → | Closure |

The Multi-Plot Story

This is the Linear Story but with two or more stories occurring simultaneously. The stories are usually linked in some way and may converge to a single ending. This is a common structure with crime stories, detective stories and similar, where two different groups, such as two or more sets of police investigators cover separate crimes. Examples of this include the American *"CSI"* television series where two investigation teams tackle two different murders. The connecting thread is commonly the head of the unit and his relationship with his staff, but may also be a common character between the two stories.

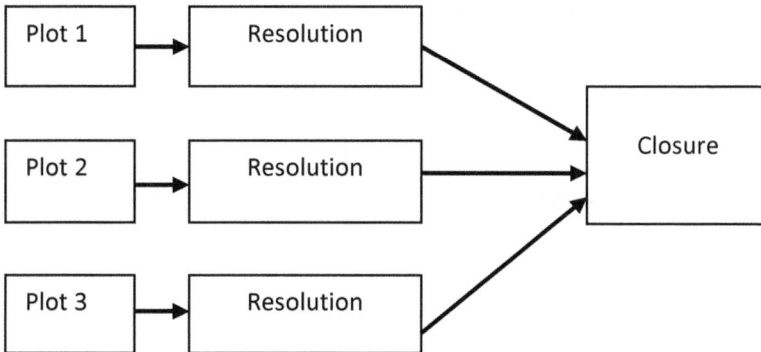

The "J-Line" Story

A common example is where some explosive or otherwise critical event occurs, usually in the present or early past at the start of the book. The timeline then reverts to some point earlier, possibly years, or maybe weeks, days or perhaps hours and another story begins that may have no obvious connection to the opening. The story proceeds to reach the point of the opening event at which the connection is established and then carries on to a conclusion.

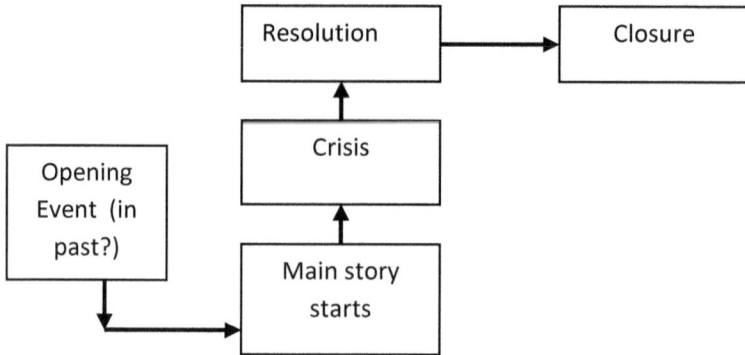

Variations on the "J-Line"

The opening event may be a prologue of an event well in the past, or even in the future. An example is my book *"The Janus Conspiracy"* which begins in Berlin in the closing days of WWII with two young Soviet officers finding treasure belonging to a Nazi General and the killing of a small group of American soldiers. The story then reverts to the present as the conspiracy unfolds and only late in the book is it made clear that the two mega-rich American industrialists leading the conspiracy are those two young Soviet officers.

Alternatively, the prologue may be in the future, matched with an epilogue also in the future. An example is one of my school project books, *"The Quest for the Locket,"* in which the prologue is a simple description of a mother putting her two infants to bed and starting to tell them a story of her childhood. The story then reverts to the present in which a group of four children have an adventure of some complexity involving the kidnapping of one of them, a seven-year old girl. At the end, the Epilogue then reveals that the mother in the Prologue was the seven-year old girl in the story.

The Converging Multiple Thread Story

This is the most complex form and is most used with British television dramas. It opens with several events, apparently all unrelated to each other. For example, one of the events is a duel between two young men possibly some decades in the past. Another is a wheelchair-bound man committing suicide and a third is a woman packing a suitcase and leaving her house in great distress. Then the main story line begins and only quite late in the tale do these unrelated events become woven together as crucial factors in the story.

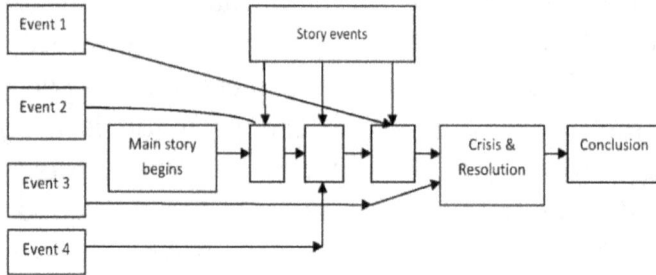

The Detective/Thriller Structure

The most common genre of book is the mystery/detective story, the "Who Dunnit." It has many common elements with the Thriller; there's a crime, there are one or more victims, there's a hero figure who will solve the crime and/or save the world and there's a perpetrator or group of villains who must be identified and brought to justice. Around all these are a number of secondary but essential characters and secondary stories, one of which is often a romance between two of the players.

This structure is shown in Diagram 10.

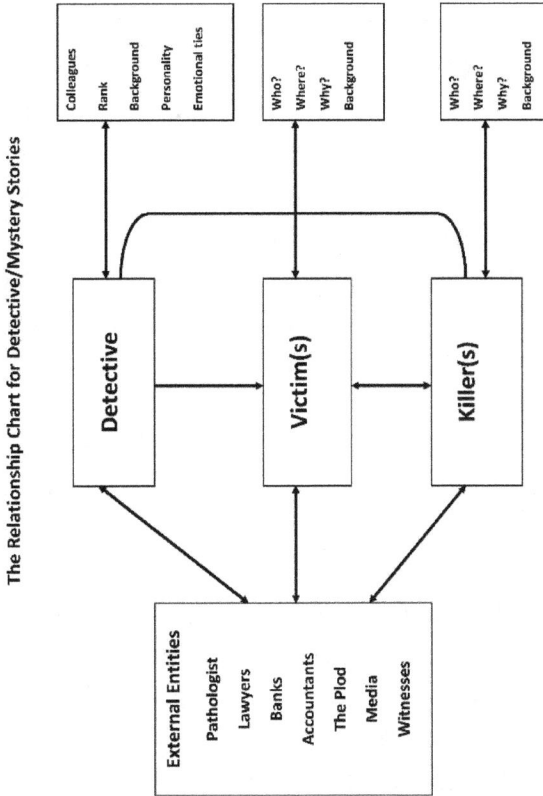

The Relationship Chart for Detective/Mystery Stories

Detective		Victim(s)		Killer(s)	
Colleagues		Who?		Who?	
Rank		Where?		Where?	
Background		Why?		Why?	
Personality		Background		Background	
Emotional ties					

External Entities

Pathologist
Lawyers
Banks
Accountants
The Plod
Media
Witnesses

Diagram 10. The Relationships and Connections

A key point is that the relationships are multi-directional and almost all-embracing. The victim, even if killed almost immediately or possibly before the story opens, is as much a key player as is the detective and killer. A relationship of some sort will exist between the victim and the detective as the investigation proceeds and delves deeply into the nature and history of the victim.

There will be a relationship, perhaps the key one between the detective and the killer (and it's always a killing or kidnap case, something that will come up a little later) even if they don't meet until almost the end. Most of the story is the "cat and mouse" game these two will play.

And of course, the relationship between the killer and the victim is the one that underlies the entire story in providing the motive to be sought by the investigators.

Around the sides of the Killer-Victim-Detective axis will be the army of bit-players, greater or smaller roles according to the story and the writer's preference, of lawyers, pathologists, other detectives and colleagues, the media and all the family friends and enemies of the main players.

There is another critically important relationship that often provides the colour to a story that makes it greater than just an intellectual exercise, and that is the relationship between the detective and his/her partner.

There is always a partner and the story doesn't work too well unless the partnership is "an Odd Couple," one more senior than the other. The writer gets a splendid opportunity to write entertaining, gripping and dramatic fiction here. Consider some of the great pairings in fiction: Holmes and Watson; Inspector Lynley and Sergeant Barbara Havers, he a titled nobleman of huge, independent wealth, she a penniless, working-class Londoner; Inspector Morse, the Oxford-educated, beer-swilling, Wagner-loving loner and Sergeant Lewis, the tee-total, Geordie family man. There are many similar partnerships, all of them providing contrast, conflict and drama over and above the murder case. However, while it is great fun to develop these relationships, the writer should aim to have the conflict impinge on the main story in some way. This may occur when the two players see events in a different way, coloured by their experience and/or culture and this helps solve the case.

A further but optional relationship can add colour to the story, and that is a romance thread. It can be one of three types:

- Between the two detectives on the case;
- Between one of the detectives and a character in the story; or
- Between two of the characters in the story.

The romance may never be complete; it could be just a running undercurrent of tension and unspoken attraction, especially if between the two detectives who try and retain a professional relationship. Again, this should only be in the story if it somehow affects the murder case and its solution. See Chapter 8 for some thoughts on the Romance Novel.

The entire story can be represented as a single structure as shown in Diagram 11.

For all the available variations in the story, this detective genre is still the most formalised and structured of the various genres available. There are good reasons for this, the primary one being that readers engage in an intellectual exercise when they read these books, a battle of wits between writer and reader. The former is trying to hide the killer's identity as long as possible and then astonish the reader with the revelation; the latter is trying to work out the identity of the killer before the writer reveals it.

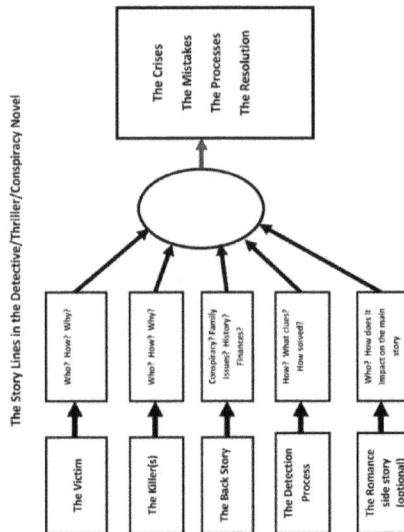

Diagram 11 – The Complete Structure

So primarily, the plot is what counts; it must be clever, imaginative and testing, and must be the key thread throughout the story despite all the other activities, relationships and sub-plots going on.

But however testing and imaginative, the rules of combat must apply! The criminal(s) and the detectives must appear in the book quite early on, certainly in the first two or three chapters in order to give the reader a fair look at the field and start laying their bets as to whodunnit.

The crime must also justify the reader's attention and interest, and that really means murder or kidnapping, possibly both. If not those, then the crime must still be of great enormity, possibly treason, or robbery if on a large-enough scale, such as a multi-million dollar bank job.

It must also be rational. Don't make a hero who can perform physical or intellectual feats that are simply not possible; an ordinary family man out for the vengeance of a gangland killing of his wife, as an example, will not, under any conditions at all, wipe out the entire criminal underworld using a wealth of sophisticated and advanced weaponry only available to the military. It's a great day-dream but it can't happen outside of Super Hero comics and American gun lobby fantasies.

The process of solving and/or resolving the crime must be logical. Police work is almost entirely a process of detailed, laborious, painstaking analysis and investigation. The odd streak of brilliance, the amazing insight, these can occur, but they are rare. The criminal will never again be identified by the cigarette stub of a brand made only for one man by a tiny tobacconist in Bermondsey (though it might occur by DNA analysis of the saliva on that stub), nor by the footprint of a pair of boots made in Tibet for a renowned world-explorer. These days are past. Instead, a breakthrough occurs from unexpected information from a "snout" (police informant), mistakes by the criminals and sometimes a stroke of luck, but the greatest majority of information comes from simple grinding investigation.

Remember also that the detective story is as much a battle of wits between reader and writer as it is between detectives and criminal. So don't reveal the answer until as late as possible. That revelation can be as dramatic as the writer can make it and can have some intriguing reactions, including violence from the criminal, unexpected revelations from others or unforeseen errors by the detectives, but the classic Agatha Christie revelations in the drawing room of the mansion house are now passé.

Nor can the detectives uncover the crime with information that is not available to the reader. Don't, for example, have the detective announce at the end that he had gone to the criminal's home town and learned some fact about the criminal or victim that explained all. It must be a fair contest between reader and writer.

And lastly, one of the absolutely unbreakable rules mentioned before – DO YOUR RESEARCH. Get the facts straight or the story loses credibility. A couple of examples here to show how I narrowly avoided embarrassment with simple situations.

In the first of my primary school projects, *"Julie Malloy and the Smugglers,"* I had two of the children in the story kidnapped and taken on a sea-going freighter, requiring rescue by the Royal Australian Navy or Coastguard. I really had no idea of how such a rescue would be achieved, what class of ship would be involved, anything at all. I called the RAN and was passed to the Media Office and spent a fascinating hour talking to a media officer who explained how the assignment would be handled and suggested that the best choice for my story would be an "Anzac" class Frigate as this could take a helicopter and thus opened up some possibilities.

Then luckily, I knew a retired RAN Lieutenant Commander who told me the rules of engagement for a boarding party, the weaponry carried, standard dress for the members of the party and similar invaluable operational facts. On his recommendation, I watched a few episodes of "Sea Patrol" and got more good stuff, and then some research on the web showed me the layout of the bridge on the "Anzac" class Frigate. More research gave me the names of all the RAN ships currently operational, so that I could select a fictional name for the one in my book and also revealed that there was at least one female commander of a frigate and thus let me have my frigate's captain be a woman (something the kids in the class had wanted!) Had I relied on what I thought I knew, I would have committed some severe blunders!

Similarly, with the other primary school projects, I needed to describe police operations in various areas.

The father of two of the girls in the class was a Senior Constable and he provided information about operations that I would never have found on the web. That leads to another recommendation – talk to the experts whenever possible! Without these conversations, some horrible mistakes would have been committed.

Chapter 6 – Playing with Time

You can't travel back in time.

Einstein said so. Hawking said so. Any number of physicists, mathematicians, cosmologists and assorted geniuses all say so. Quantum theory suggests that it might, under some circumstances and with deeper understanding of the forces that created the Universe, be possible to travel back in time, but there are no signs of how that might come about.

So you can't travel back in time.

You can go forward. Just sit still and you travel forward. Fly at massive speed around the world like a satellite and time travels at a different rate than on the ground, which is something the satellite navigation systems have to take into account. Fly out to the edge of the solar system at a significant fraction of the speed of light, turn round and come back and you'll find the people you knew are years older while you have aged much less.

But you can't travel back in time.

However, there may be a perfectly satisfactory alternative. It's called writing fiction.

Very few novels begin at a set point in time and proceed in the same time zone to the end. Devices like prologues, which may take place in the past, the present of the future, flash-backs to events in the past or flash-forwards to events at some future time are all common. Intelligent use of these devices can make for a colourful, complex story but just as easily, create an incomprehensible mess.

The standard sequence, shown before in Chapter 5 for the most simple story is as follows.

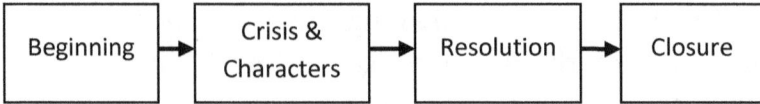

But this can be varied by some parts of the story taking place in the past or the future, as follows.

The Main Sections of a story

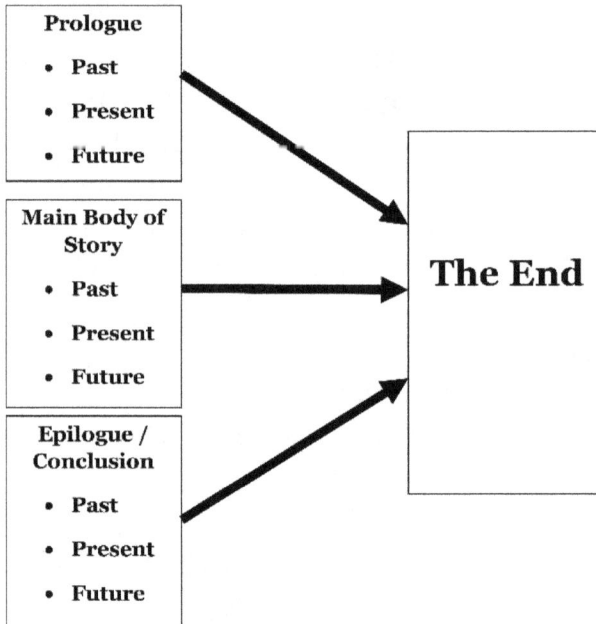

Note that any part of the story can take place in the past, the present or the future. While the most common structure is to have a prologue in the past, the main story in the present and the epilogue in the present or future, note these examples in two of the school book projects:

Some Examples of Children's Stories in Multiple Time Zones

The Quest for the Locket	The Star of the Yshan Kings
Prologue –	No prologue, story starts with twin brother and sister coming to the school as their parents have moved to the area. They make friends with three kids at the school
Young mother putting two children to bed, tells them a story of when she was a little girl	
	Discovery that they are the children of the Galactic Emperor and they are on Earth looking for the mysterious Star, a strange crystal that has guided the Royal House for 5,000 years.
Mainline –	
Story of several kids at school, one gets kidnapped and held for ransom.	**Flashback 12 years**
	The twins are just weeks old and the Emperor's brother is told that the Emperor is dead in an accident and his son, The Crown Prince is missing. Then the discovery that the Star is also missing. The brother must become the Emperor.
For some reason, the Army sends an Intelligence Officer (the father of one of the boys to work with the police	
It turns out that the kidnapped girl is the boy's sister and their mother is the estranged husband of the Army Officer and an international criminal	**Mainline**
	The hunt for the Star continues, the twin sister is revealed as a conspirator with her Uncle
Flashback several years	**Flashback 5,000 Years**
Story shows the final marriage breakup and why the siblings are separated.	The world is dying, the Yshan Tribe is almost wiped out, a mysterious being gives the leader the Star which will save them. It does, over the centuries the Star's guidance makes the Yshan tribe the royal family of a Galactic Empire.
Mainline -	**Mainline**
Final hunt for the criminals and their capture	The Star is found, one of the kids is revealed as the rightful Heir, everybody goes to Yshan for the Coronation
Epilogue –	
Young mother (who was the little girl who was kidnapped) finishes putting the kids to bed	

In *"The Quest for the Locket"* the prologue is in the future (or perhaps the present), the mainline story is in the present (or perhaps the past), there is a flashback further back to the past, a return to the mainline story and the epilogue continues where the prologue began.

In the sci-fi story, *"The Star of the Yshan Kings,"* the story begins in the present, there is a flashback to a time twelve years earlier, a return to the mainline story in the present, a second flashback to a time 5,000 years before and a return to the mainline story.

Controlling this movement between time zones requires careful control, but when done well adds considerable texture and interest to the story.

Some examples of mixing time sequences:

Some Example of Story Structures

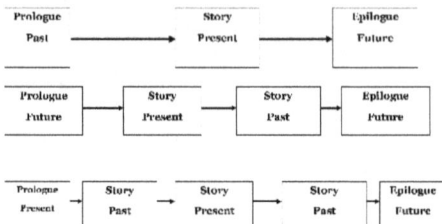

Prologue		Story		Epilogue
Past →		Present →		Future

Prologue	Story	Story	Epilogue
Future	Present	Past	Future

Prologue	Story	Story	Story	Epilogue
Present	Past	Present	Past	Future

At a more complex level, it can be like this:

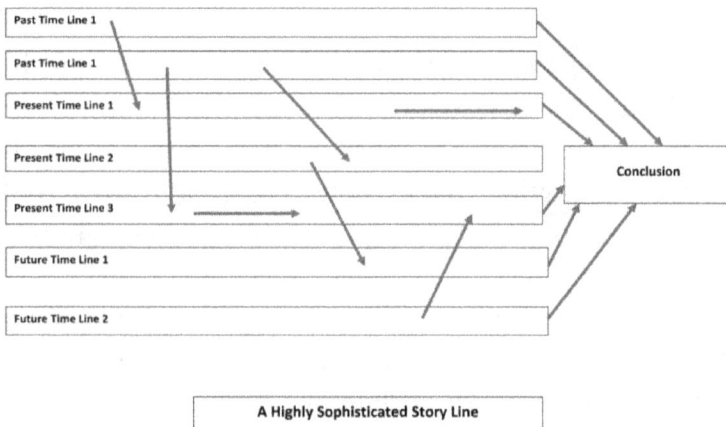

Past Time Line 1

Past Time Line 1

Present Time Line 1

Present Time Line 2

Conclusion

Present Time Line 3

Future Time Line 1

Future Time Line 2

A Highly Sophisticated Story Line

Chapter 7 – Science Fiction

One of the main reasons I love writing Sci-Fi is because it gives you the most creative options of all, designing a complete civilisation and a whole world. The first time I did this with a group was with the extraordinary class of young people at St Joseph's High School with whom I wrote the Mickie Dalton Trilogy. It was early on in the project and to that date we had spent most of the time reviewing the first manuscript which I had written before the project had begun. I gave the class a challenge, to suggest a civilisation that we could develop as a fully-fledged environment for one adventure in the book. Several came up with ideas, but the one that intrigued me most was the one from James Goddard who suggested a civilisation that was technologically savvy, knew about space-travel, communicated with other species, etc., and yet practiced Inca or Druid-like blood sacrifices at home.

The class really got into this one and it was the first time I encountered the extraordinary level of imagination and creativity that children (they were all 13 at the time) can achieve when given the freedom to fly. The end result made for a wonderful chapter in Book II, *"The Many Galaxies of Mickie Dalton"* where they encounter the weird civilisation of Drudyenko.

One of my favourite examples though, was where we developed another complete civilisation of the three-armed Kamotari, a very large, boisterous and energetic species that had evolved with three arms, one on the right being huge, powerful and muscular, the other two on the left, smaller and delicate.

Designing a civilisation is about as God-like an act of Creation as one can enjoy. There are so many factors to consider; what is the political system? What sorts of sports would develop? Given that physical shape, what sort of rules of society would develop? How would cities be designed? What sort of diet would such a people have? As with the development of people, not everything we came up with was specifically mentioned in the book, but it all helped to produce a civilisation and people that came alive and helped further the Homeric Odyssey that is the Mickie Dalton Trilogy. When I summarised the results in Diagram 12, we had a race of the Kamotari that was quite complex.

THE KAMOTARI

ABOUT 7 FOOT ON AVERAGE, HEAVY BUILD, RIGHT ARM
POWERFUL, 2 LEFT ARMS DELICATE & LIGHT

POLITICAL —— CITY STATES, LOOSE FEDERATIONS BY
SYSTEM   CONTINENTS. MIX OF HEREDITARY KINGS,
              ELECTED GOVERNMENTS

SPORTS — FAST, VIOLENT, CONTACT SPORTS
         "PROTASKORP" — MIX OF BASKETBALL &
         AUSSIE RULES

DIET — NEEDS HIGH PROTEIN, OMNIVEROUS,
       BUT MOSTLY MEAT

SOCIAL NORMS— KEEP THE RIGHT ARM (FIGHTING ARM)
UNDER CLOAK, BUT AVAILABLE AS NEEDED
EATING IN COMPANY—USE LEFT ARMS ONLY

FAIRLY ADVANCED TECHNOLOGY— KNOWS SPACE TRAVEL.
HI-GRAVITY WORLD— MASSIVE SOURCE OF GEMSTONES,
SO WEALTHY.

INDUSTRIES — MINING, ENGINEERING & ASSOCIATED
             TECHNOLOGIES

BE CAREFUL WITH SMALLER SPECIES Z CHILDREN
—TRANSIT LANES FOR SUCH ON SIDEWALKS

REVERSED (AS HUMAN LEFTIES) SHAPE INVARIABLY
GIFTED, CREATIVE & ATHLETIC, TINY FRACTION
OF POPULATION, REVERED IN ALL WALKS.

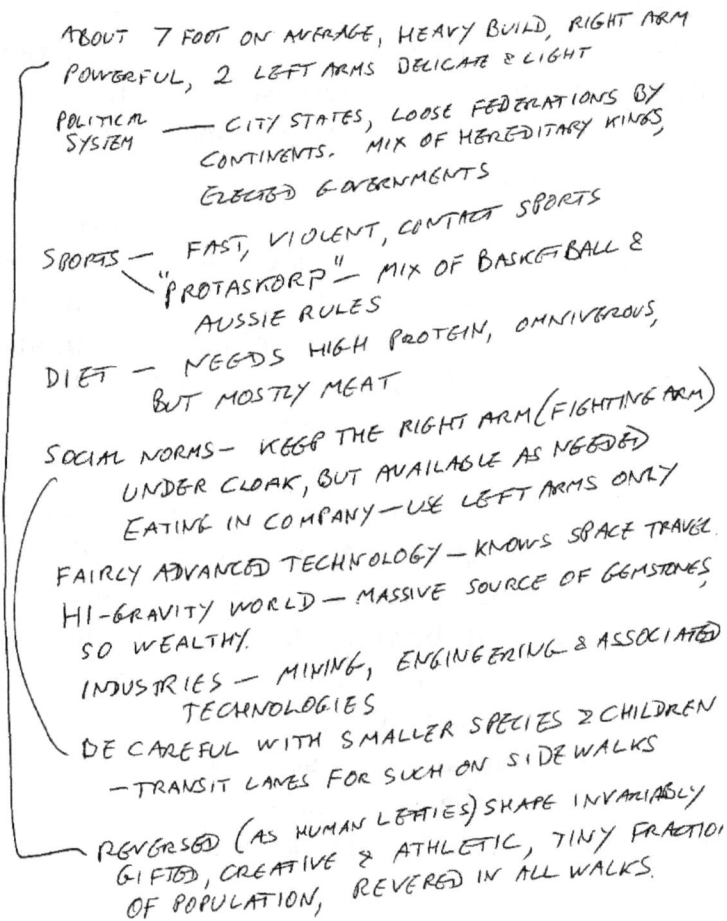

Diagram 12 – The World of the Kamotari

Being essentially huge and physical, we assumed they originally were warlike and combative, so a tight government format was unlikely. Instead, large city states with hereditary kings were loosely assembled into federations within the continents with elected representatives for regions.

Sports would be violent, contact sports. "Protaskorp" was the main game, a mix of basketball and Australian Rules Football played on a football field-sized oval before crowds of a quarter million or more, with a 20-kilo ball that is passed and thrown to a scoring area with minor and major points according to accuracy.

Social norms would reflect the innate violence of the society, requiring that children and smaller species must be protected at all times, with transit lanes for such on the sidewalks to ensure they do not have to mix it with the constant heavy contacts between the crowds. Because the right arm was the original fighting arm and still used in sports, good taste mandated that it would be covered by a cloak in social conditions, but could be easily brought into use if required.

It's a heavy-gravity world that has produced massive amounts of high-quality gemstones and these provide the greatest export to the rest of the universe, so the wealth is high and industry is well-developed, mostly mining and engineering. Artistic skills are not valued nor commonly practiced.

The equivalent of the human "Lefty" is the "Gryasvert" a mirror-image individual so that the fighting arm is on the left. Such individuals are invariably superb athletes and intellects and in huge demands in all walks of life, most ending up in the law and politics.

One could go on at great length, but the Kamotari are one of my favourite creations from the Mickie Dalton project and I moved this section into Book 1 even though we developed it during later stages.

To summarise; the factors to be considered when designing an alien species and its civilisation are:

1. Evolution – from what animals or entities did this species evolve? It will be key to how they have developed. What is their procreation system, life-cycle and duration? Consider my "Harliya" in the Mickie Dalton series, a race of tiny tree-dwellers who live only six to eight years and reach adulthood within 18 months, and yet are highly intelligent, philosophical, spiritual and accept their primary role on the food chain to a giant species of carnivore.

2. Diet - what is the standard essential diet, has it changed over the centuries, has it changed under the impact of meeting alien species?

3. Language invariably reflects culture. If creating speech in an alien race, spend a lot of time thinking how a language might evolve and what shape and sound it might have. This also applies to place names in alien civilisations. On my planet Mayoowani, I have a race of gentle people, somewhat Hawaiian in style. So my place names, people names and language all tend to a rather soft, smooth, mellow sound to reflect the culture. My race of X'Kasxi

evolved from large lizards; their names and language tend to a hissing, multi-syllabic structure. A capable linguist could do far better than I have, I'm certain, but it is at least consistent.

4. Social norms – how does these people live? What is considered "normal" in daily life? What sort of industry, technology, business levels exist, if any at all?

5. What is the political structure? Consider as part of this, the world's geography and geology, climate, atmosphere, and so on. Are there large continental masses or smaller island-type structures, or both? Are they spread around the whole planet or concentrated in equatorial regions. What impact will this have on culture and society?

6. Arts – are there any? What sort of building structures exist and how will they reflect the shape and size of the individuals?

One can go on and on in this development and this only touches on planet-based physical creatures, so far only mammalian. What about species evolved from (say) birds or lizards or even insects, with high intellectual capacities? How would all the factors above differ with such creatures? And what about species that are not planet-bound and exist in (say) electrical or gaseous form? These present a particularly challenging exercise in designing a civilisation.

My race of super-intelligent massive spiders, the Zlan was barely developed in the Mickie Dalton Trilogy, I feel. I could have gone a lot further, though at least I had a family structure, pairs mated for life, there was a "Council of the Zlan," but I didn't take this any further. Should I ever undertake a redevelopment of the Trilogy, I think there would be some further work on the species of the Zlan.

Not only does sci-fi provide the greatest opportunities for creative development, it has arguably the widest variations in category.

Categories of Sci-Fi

1. Invasion of Earth;
2. New Planet Colonisation;
3. Inter-Planetary Warfare;
4. Star-Trek adventures; ("Cowboys in Space")
5. Time Travel;
6. New Technology:
   - New power source;
   - New device;
   - New transportation capability;
   - New Communication capability.
7. New Human capability (e.g., telepathy, teleportation, telekinesis);
8. Alien Monster(s);
9. Ecological disaster;
10. Post-Nuclear world;
11. Post Other Disaster World.
    - Medical;
    - Asteroid Collision;
    - Population explosion/implosion.

> Categories 9-11 tend to be mostly "Survivalist" stories.

Some Sci-fi Conventions:

- Faster-than-light travel: this is essential if other worlds/civilisations must be encountered because of the hundreds and thousands or even millions of light years that exist between solar systems. Common ways of evading current physical laws that nothing can exceed the speed of light include alternative universes such as worm-holes, hyperspace and similar. Older stories often were about colony ships that travelled at sub-light speeds and took generations to get there, a story in itself.

- Telepathy as a means of communication, commonly not bound by physical laws (see above) and instantaneous across infinite distances. However, Quantum Physics now indicates that instantaneous communication across infinite distances is theoretically possible by technical means.

- Alternate Universes; one that might be identical to our own but where history has evolved differently, (e.g., Hitler won WWII) or where physical and other laws may be different.

General Comments

A common view in literature is that Sci-Fi provides a platform from which to view our own society and its strengths, weaknesses and characteristics. It also reflects our world view; the hey-day of alien invasion stories was during the Cold War when the aliens really represented the Communists and their perceived threat to the West. Such stories have given way to new styles of adventure with the end of the Cold War.

Science and technology are NOT the central factor – they merely provide the key to the story. The central issue is the effects that science/technology have on society and individuals.

A fact – every technological development of the last few decades has at some stage been forecast in sci-fi works and usually ridiculed at the time. A prime example – Arthur C. Clarke's forecast in 1945 that a series of geo-stationary orbiting satellites could provide global communications, television and navigation services. It was widely ridiculed by many scientists.

In 1986, an article appeared in a scientific journal stating that 90% of the inventions of the 20th Century had yet to be made. It turned out to be very nearly correct, overestimating the percentage by only one or two points.

Arthur C. Clarke again: *"If an eminent scientist says something is impossible, he is almost certainly wrong. If an eminent scientist says something is possible, he is quite certainly correct".*

Some Iconic Sci-Fi Books

These are four of the best-known works in the genre and are listed here to give some idea of the type of stories and their scope.

I Robot (Isaac Asimov)

A series of short stories written in 1939-40, eventually merged into a lengthy novel about the development and history of robots some time in the far future. These are not the metallic, clumsy creations of popular concept. Asimov's robots are indistinguishable from humans, but built on steel skeletons and engineered to have far superior strength and speed than humans. Asimov introduced two concepts that have remained a standard in all such tales. The first is the Positronic Brain, the second, "The Three Laws of Robotics" that have become incorporated in advanced technology thinking. These are:

1. A robot may not injure a human being or, through inaction, allow a human being to come to harm.
2. A robot must obey any orders given to it by human beings, except where such orders would conflict with the First Law.
3. A robot must protect its own existence as long as such protection does not conflict with the First or Second Law.

The genius behind this is recognised by all scientists.

Foundation Series (Isaac Asimov)

Perhaps the most famous series of four books (more after the series merged with the "I Robot" series in recent years). A Galactic Empire exists, apparently at the peak of its greatness. The main character is a scientist, Hari Seldon who has developed a speciality known as "Psychohistory." I think of it as Epidemiology on steroids, the science of predicting future history when based on populations of hundreds of BILLIONS of people. Seldon predicts the fall of the Galactic Empire and a period of 30,000 years of darkness before a new empire arises. He creates the Foundation, supposedly a record-keeping operation taking up the resources of a whole planet, dedicated to recording all science to ease the return of the new empire when it arises. But unknown to anyone, he creates a Second Foundation, hidden "at the other end of the Galaxy" with an entirely different agenda. Using Psychohistory, he predicts a series of events over the next 40,000 years and what to do to overcome the crises. The story covers the multi-thousand year hunt for the Second Foundation, its own history and the eventual fall of the Empire and the rise of the new one.

Cities in Flight (James Blish)

Blish creates two astounding developments; discovery of gravity control which allows an object of any mass to be lifted from Earth, and the *"anti-agathics,"* a series of drugs that block ageing. Whole cities lift off earth and begin to fly around the Galaxy as migrant workers. The primary city in the story is

New York and its Mayor, John Amalfi has become perhaps the best-known character in the sci-fi genre. Amalfi lives 1000 years through the trilogy. Blish avoids one problem by ignoring it! The cities cannot exceed the speed of light but the stories take New York all over the Galaxy which is 100,000 light years on its long axis.

Dune (Frank Herbert)

Herbert creates a complete planet, Arakis, a desert world almost totally without water. But Arakis contains the greatest treasure in the Galaxy (and this is also a Galactic Empire scenario), the Spice Melange, which extends life, increases intelligence, health but also psychic and spiritual powers. It is only found on Arakis but mining it is a dangerous business because of the Giant Worms, creatures over 100 metres long who live in the sand and attack any mechanic object or creature that emits any rhythmic noise, either by drilling or even walking. Arakis has its natives, and Herbert has created a society that is based on Desert Bedouin cultures. The story includes a generations-long war between the Harkonnens and the Atreides, two noble houses, a mysterious and powerful female society, the *Bene Gesserit*, and galactic space travel using the "Navigators," humans who live on a massive diet of the spice and evolve into bizarre species utterly beyond human comprehension who take ships across the Galaxy by "folding" space. The series went over a series of books, tracking the life of Paul Atreides, the man who came to rule Arakis and took over the Galaxy by controlling the Worms and the Spice.

Chapter 8 – The Romance Novel

I'm a bloke; I don't do Romance Novels.

Such was my view until I started looking at the essential elements of this genre to round out the writing classes I taught. Then I realised that most of my books, even the Young Adults *"Mickie Dalton Trilogy"* had a romance element to them. The only exceptions are the primary school projects!

Like every other genre, the Romance genre has various categories but regardless of which one, the romance IS the story; there's little else but some form of vehicle to carry the relationship between the lovers. One example of these is the Harlequin or Mills & Boone style and these I cannot write. There are historical romances, romantic thrillers, sci-fi romances, but with all these, the romance is the key thread. But in the real world, the attraction between the sexes is a constant and will therefore likely appear during a thriller, murder or mystery story but not be the dominant thread. The romance theme does, however, provide extra colour and dimensions to the primary story.

Like the other genres, there is a model that provides the essential structure and this is shown in Diagram 13.

If you are writing for the above-mentioned Harlequin operation, the structure is far more tightly constrained and aspiring writers should contact the organisation for their guidelines.

The Standard Structure for a Romance

The Man
Appearance;
Background
History
Status, etc

The Woman
Appearance;
Background
History
Status, etc

Initial Hostility (Optional) → **Resolution**

The Idyllic Phase

The Crisis
Friends
Family
Religion
Culture
History
Ex-Spouses
Habits
Hobbies
Tastes
Activities
etc

The Resolution

Happy Ever After

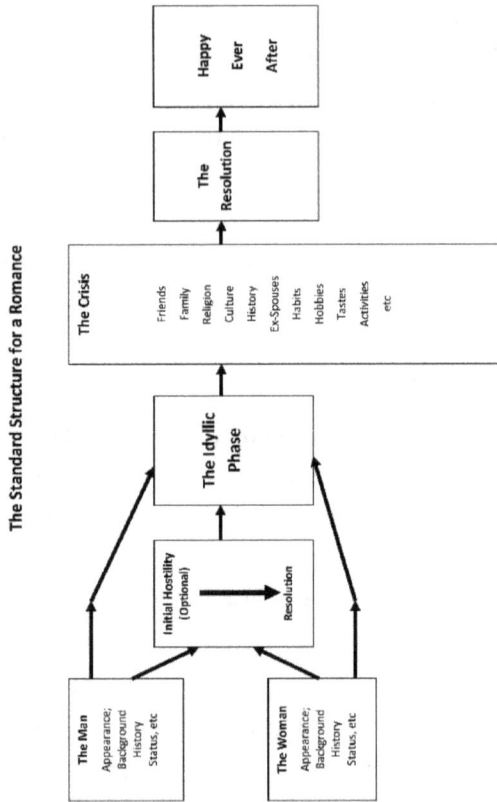

Diagram 13 – The Structure of the Romance Novel

A common theme in the romance is that the participants initially experience hostility for some reason. This may be cultural, personal, for reasons of career, or competition but the hostility will initially override and hide the mutual attraction.

This initial hurdle is soon overcome and the lovers enter the Idyllic Phase, regardless of whatever else is going on.

But a Crisis will arrive, taking one or more of the examples shown in the diagram. Not only is this stressful to the lovers, it will have a damaging effect on the main story line. The Crisis must be resolved, but whether by the lovers settling their differences or agreeing to return to a platonic relationship (as might be the case if the romance is developing between the two detectives) is up to the writer's preference and/or the logic of the situation.

As mentioned in an earlier chapter, a romance thread in a thriller or detective story should only appear if it moves the story along and adds an extra dimension to the novel. And if it does appear, my recommendation is to keep it rational – no heaving bosoms, no pink-tipped white hillocks of delight, no engorged manhoods, just a man and a woman experiencing a mutual attraction and growing love for each other. Nor is there any need at all for graphic sexual encounters. All that stuff detracts from the real story.

All other factors apply that apply in the other genres – the characters should be interesting, dialogue snappy and intelligent and the story should flow. Whether the story has the standard Happily Ever After ending, or a sad one (*"Romeo and Juliet"*), a frustrated one (*"Bridges of Madison County"*) or a "Put on Hold" ending (for example where the couple hold off any further developments for personal or professional reasons) the rules of story-telling still apply.

Chapter 9 – Writing for Kids

"Not only is the universe stranger than we imagine, it is stranger than we can imagine."

Though sometimes attributed to Sir Arthur Stanley Eddington an astrophysicist of the early 20th century, this quotation seems to be derived from a statement by J.B.S. Haldane in *Possible Worlds and Other Papers* (1927), p. 286: *"The Universe is not only queerer than we suppose, but queerer than we can suppose."*

After working on six books written with children between the ages of seven and thirteen, I make my own version: *"The minds of children are not just more creative and imaginative than we suppose, they are more creative and imaginative than anyone CAN suppose."*

I don't know at what point we kill off this genius in our social and educational system. I suspect that we don't fully destroy it, we just suppress it and force it to run and hide until released by some rare forces.

I believe that the process I brought to the school projects was one of those forces. Given the freedom from ridicule and rejection and the encouragement to produce ideas that a well-trained facilitator provides, the environment we had in our projects resulted in some startling ideas. Just as critical, I realised that the kids can cope with and grasp concepts and ideas way above what current society believes possible or advisable.

During a lunch break at Byabarra School during the project to write *"The Secret of Yuri Kirilenko,"* I had taken out the *"Mickie Dalton Trilogy"* (written for the 12-18 age group) to show to the Principal. As we conversed, I saw that one nine-year old girl had picked up the first book and was deeply into it, so much so that the Principal had to call her name three times before the child realised. I left the books with her and the child read all three during the week and was enthralled by them. Others have since followed that example.

So my first and major recommendation for when writing for any children above the age of seven or eight is: place no ceiling on what you think they will cope with. The child's mind can rise to cope with almost anything and understand it.

What you should watch, however, is the language you use. Don't talk down to them, but don't apply a vocabulary that will be above their heads.

There is a wonderful opportunity to teach the kids something in your book. During the *"Yuri Kirilenko"* project, one girl suggested that Yuri was a foreign prince. This idea was popular and as the group had already said Yuri was Georgian, I took the opportunity to talk a little about the old Soviet regime and what it had replaced. It was not long before the group had adopted the whole concept and made Yuri a direct descendent of Czar Nicholas II, the last Czar of the old Russian Empire. This was written into the story and now at least one group of children (and those who read the book eventually) know something of Russian and Soviet history.

If you see the opportunity, sneak in some educational elements in your book!

The second recommendation is to make the characters in your book good role models for the children who will be your reader. I try and have my fictional kids display at least:

- Courage;
- Resourcefulness;
- Energy;
- Curiosity; and
- Intelligence.

I also aim to have them speak well and display tolerance and consideration. I realise this could make my characters horrible little "goodies" but this can be avoided by having these qualities displayed by the characters during stressful and dangerous situations without the point being hammered home in any moralising way. Nor should this be taken to deny that kids can be naughty, rude and inconsiderate, but that happens in the process of learning and kids will always test the envelope of what they can get away with.

So, to summarise my two recommendations:

1. Place no ceiling on your expectation of what the children can cope with. My groups of 7-12 year olds have so far had no difficulty at all in coping with (among a lot of other things): revolution, murder, kidnapping, killing in self-defence, alien life forms whether benign or malignant, quantum physics concepts,

> inadequate or even hostile parents, international espionage, and much more.

2. Make the characters in the story good role models for them to follow in behaviour, morality and language but do so subtly; as I have said earlier, *DON'T PREACH!!*

Illustrating the Book

This is a completely personal matter for the writer. I like to illustrate books for the 7-11 age group with simple drawings that break up the text and perhaps

keep the story focused. For the Young Adult set (12-18), I don't include illustrations. Both these approaches result from what I found the children preferred. There are no illustrations in adult stories and I think the 12-18 year-olds see themselves as adult and thus they emulate that standard.

The style of illustrations is also entirely a personal choice. For the first of the primary school books,

"Julie Malloy and the Smugglers," we were fortunate that Sue Ahern, the parent of two of the girls in the project team was an accomplished artist and produced a delightful series of drawings in a 1950s "Retro Enid Blyton" style that seemed to fit the book perfectly. This is one example:

With the next two books we tried something different after having problems finding an artist who didn't need paying. We took photographs of scenes we wanted, took occasional downloads off the Internet then used Photoshop to modify them, and finally pushed the pictures through a software product that converted photographs to drawings.

So in the book about Yuri Kirilenko, a posed shot of four kids from the class, a picture of Car Nicholas II downloaded off the Internet, some magic of Photoshop and we had a drawing of four kids looking at a portrait. I doubt I'll use an Illustrator again, but in future projects, I'll be far more precise and planned in setting up the shots. But the bonus feature of this approach was the even greater involvement of the children in the process of writing and producing a book. Having the parents and teachers involved adds a further bonus to the project.

If the book requires illustrations to entertain and educate as part of the book's "Payoff Concept," a higher grade of illustration may be required. I produced one cartoon book, "Flatulent Tales; the Adventures of Gilbert the Farting Mouse" as an entertainer for the 6-11 age group. But I couldn't help myself and was sneaky by aiming to improve the reading skills of the audience. Under the guidance of a psychologist specialising in children's creativity, I wrote the stories more at a 12-15 level of writing. With Robert's advice in mind, that the children would read more intently if entertained by the stories and by the pictures, I had a local artist, Holly Cox produce an exquisite set of drawings that cause guffaws among children and adults alike. This is Gilbert protecting the house from burglars by doing what Gilbert did best.

I also had a professional pair of CDs produced with all the stories beautifully recorded together with the requisite sound effects. Overall, the effect was exactly what I wanted: children read the books together with the CD, were amused, intrigued, charmed and fully engaged, and without realising it, absorbed a higher level of reading than their nominal age group.

For the "Littlies," the children under seven, the illustrations are the primary tool to enchant the children and the text, while important, is by far the smaller part of the book. Those I have seen are anything from 20-50 pages long with only about 2,000 to 3,000 words, providing a fairly simple narrative to the illustrations, which are colourful and exquisite. Keep the vocabulary fairly simple but ensure the grammar and sentence structure are accurate because the kids will absorb like sponges what you have written.

Chapter 10 - Controlling the Story -
Sequence of Events

Paul Simon sang a wonderful song some years ago entitled *"Fifty Ways to Leave your Lover."* There are probably just as many ways for a writer's fans to leave, but the key ones, apart from writing badly, involve losing control of the story, the sequence of events and objects. I cannot teach you anything at all about writing well, but minimising the control problem is fortunately quite simple. This section covers the first factor, the sequence of events, the second is covered in the following section and is equally critical.

There are several problems involved with losing control of the sequence. One is simply trying to find the place where you wrote a particular piece should you wish to modify or move it. Much time can be spent reading through many pages, or using the search facility when there is no unique word or phrase that you can recall in the specific section on which to base your search. This wastes time from productive writing and raises the irritation level which is a serious creativity killer.

The other problem is that it is easy to write initially that event 1 is followed by event 2 followed by event 3, and just as easy to write subsequently that event 2 is followed by event 1. At its worst, that can ruin the entire story if you have based a complex plot on a series of events and got it wrong. The reader closes the book and switches on the television and may never return to you. I know of at least two well-known writers who will never get me to read their works again because of this failure.

The solution is simple; log the story events. It doesn't need a complex description of each event, just a few key words and be sure to keep them within chapter headings. This way, you can find the section you may wish to modify just by looking at a single sheet. My preference is to use Microsoft Excel for this purpose.

What this also facilitates is that you can keep track of the story, especially if you have had to leave it for a lengthy interval. Otherwise, you may have to read through your entire manuscript to get your mind back into gear of what you have done so far. You can also track the developments closely. For example, my sci-fi hero Mickie Dalton develops the powers of his species as he matures. I had to make very certain that he did not use one in a crisis before he had been shown to have developed it.

However, it is absolutely critical that you modify your event log at any time you change the sequence of events in the book itself.

An example of my event log for *"The Many Worlds of Mickie Dalton"* is shown in Diagram 14.

Sample Control Document

Chapter 1 - Mickie at Home	**Chapter 12 - Speaking with a Speaker**
Misery at home	Discussion with Speaker 356
Strange dreams, first mental contact	Talk about the Spider Contact
Called by Allie to the park	Unable to contact Spiders
Chapter 2 - Close Encounters	First meeting with Eater of Souls
Riot in park	**Chapter 13 - Shuramee**
Attacked by hoons	Lesson from Albert re Shuramee
Saved by strange appearance	Kids explore the forest
Grant carries him to shuttle	Finding the Treasure Vault
Learns he's not human	Finding the Kamotar 4 Script
Mission set to discover his identity	Finding the word "Pfafth"
Chapter 3 - The End of a World	**Chapter 14 - The Space Dwellers**
Mickie leaves home	Mickie tells his friends about Pfafth
Goes to the shuttle	Meeting the Space Dwelling species
Learns about the Ship & Kaloti	The Family sends greetings to Pfafth
Chapter 4 - The Voyage begins	**Chapter 15 - Some Self-Discoveries**
Reaches the ship	Contacts the Spiders
Meets the Captain	The Pfafth as Spiders' controllers
Shown his quarters	With Grant & Allie - first empathy
Watches entry to hyperspace	Speaker agrees it's a new power
Ship's mission explained	**Chapter 16 - The World of the Kamotari**
Chapter 5 - The Learning Continues	Planet-Fall, meet Zhumaton
Has translator	Tour of City - ref gold and diamonds
Meets Albert the Computer	See Gryvestra
Learns about the Spiders	Trip to the Mural with Kamotar 4 script
Albert's lesson about Spiders	Lunch, the game of Protaskorp
First encounter with the Blackness	The Smegandri attack
Chapter 6 - Making New Friends	Mickie connects with a hostage
Taken to the school	Attack on the Smegandri
Meets the other three	Mickie hurts the Smegandri
Introduced to Sheekmetter	Spiders deny assisting
Introduced to Loopies	**Chapter 17 - Learning the Speakers' Art**
Galactic Geography lesson	Talk with parents
Chats with friends	Practice session
Chapter 7 - The World of the Spiders	Briefing from Speaker 356
Second encounter with Blackness	More practice - identifying species
Meets first X'Kasxi	Discovery of blocked mind on ship
First conversation with Speaker 356	Entity vanishes

Diagram 14 – Sequence Chart from "Many Worlds"

Chapter 11 – Controlling the Story – People and Objects

I have read books where a character arrives in a black suit, but somehow during the ensuing scene, puts his wallet back into his sports jacket. Or his shoes change from brown loafers to black lace-ups. People have driven up in a green MGB and departed in their red Jaguar. Women have appeared on the scene in a little black cocktail dress with their hair up and at some point tossed their curls and turned sharply so that their skirts flew. People have been six foot tall in one chapter and five foot ten in another. He's called Jack in Chapter Six and Jacques in Chapter Ten because the writer decided to make his English hero into a French Canadian at some point in the story and somehow forgot the earlier bits.

You mustn't do it. It's a killer to your writing career unless you have some other factor that somehow overcomes this silliness, like being immensely rich or have written the Harry Potter books. (Not that JK Rowling made these mistakes.)

As with the logging of events, log people and objects as well. As soon as you create a character, log their entrance with a small description of their appearance, name, age, general characteristics and anything else that may be critical, such as the manner of dress if that is to be mentioned. But be warned. Every writer knows the experience of introducing a character to help move the story along, not intending the newcomer to be anything but a linkage, but finding that character taking a significant role in the book. So even if you didn't intend that to happen, if it starts to occur, do the entire whiteboard exercise and create a fully three-dimensional form and history to augment the initial sketch.

Log everything. If the character is wearing a ring that may be relevant to the story, describe it. If he has a boomerang on his lounge wall, log it. And if it has been worth mentioning at all with any emphasis, at some stage ensure that the boomerang plays a part in the story. Don't introduce any item unless you intend to use it somewhere in the story.

Log the person's ownership of a green Austin Healey Sprite and always check back before he or she drives off or arrives in a car, unless it's a new car or somebody's else's car in which case be sure to mention that fact in the book. If he drinks scotch, you may want to name the brand and then stick with it unless there is a deliberate change somewhere, e.g., the hero goes off Glenfiddich and turns to Laphroaig as "his" scotch, but then be sure to say so and why. Or if you don't want to name the brand, ensure that if he drinks single-malt as a preference, he sticks to it and only drinks a blend under protest, and doesn't suddenly switch to gin. If her ex-husband is called Harold, ensure he is *always* called Harold and doesn't become Fred in Chapter Ten.

With sci-fi it's even more critical if you have created place or people names or items such as a special drink or device. I made that mistake with a drink I called *"Sle 'Ach"* in the Mickie Dalton first book and got it wrong a few times before a proof-reader saw it. Log the place names, items, people names etc., immediately you introduce them and always refer back to the log before repeating the reference.

Diagram 15 shows the log I created as I wrote *"The Many Worlds of Mickie Dalton."*

Another thing to get right is your geography. If one location is east of the point of action, don't have the hero drive west to get to it, nor have it be 300 kilometres away in Chapter Four and 500 kilometres in Chapter Ten. For the Mickie Dalton Trilogy, I created an entire map of the Universe, at least to be certain about the distances between Galaxies, and some were very much further than others. I also made sure that I logged which species inhabited which Galaxy.

Michie's Mother smokes Players Extra Mild
His Father — Jack
Michie's room — bed, kitchen table & chair
Allie — dark hair, pretty, wide mouth
Grant — tall, thin, protruding ears, bent nose
The drink — Sle 'Ach
In suitcase, he puts Aust. football jersey, books — Blish
"Flying Cities" Asimov "Foundation"
Allie & Grant are from KALAMOS
Captain & Crew are KALOTI
SHIP — 1 km+ long, 500ms wide
ship clothing — one-piece tunic
Crew of 50 Kaloti, 360 people on board
Captain — classic "Grey" — 3m tall, speech sounds
    like cello
Cabins are on Deck 37, Region 12
Cassoleans — pale blue skin, no nose, red eyes
His cabin — light blue carpet, 2 coffee tables
    couches, full bookshelf, Atlas
    bedroom on one side, TV & stereo set
X 'KASXI — other crew members

Diagram 15 - Initial Log for "Many Worlds"

Chapter 12 – Some Thoughts on Research

My main comment on research is that you can't really do too much, but you can certainly do too little.

Another of the fifty ways to lose your readers is to get your facts wrong. I have already talked about British writer Dick Francis who I believe set the standards for research and his meticulous accuracy in everything he wrote. Wilbur Smith is another, a writer who gets everything right and in the process, grips the readers and holds them in his story until the end.

On the other hand, there are some horrible examples of slapdash work, assumptions and sheer ignorance that aren't checked. There is one world-famous writer of popular thrillers who will never get me to open his pages again because I read one of his books in which he describes a helicopter taking off and he writes *"The pilot's hands were busy on the controls as they lifted off the whaling ship."*

Er..... no. I have had some helicopter pilot experience (though I am not a qualified rotary wing pilot) and the one thing that is very obvious is that the pilot's movements are almost undetectable almost all the time. The left hand is on the collective lever and throttle down by the left side and the right hand on the cyclic lever between the knees. The controls are so sensitive that only the most minute movements are required except in such emergencies as an engine failure when the pilot will disengage the rotor from the engine and move the collective lever down sharply. But when lifting off? No, hardly a muscle-twitch to be seen.

He lost me then and there with possibly a thousand more pilots in that one sentence.

Another world-famous writer wrote of somebody in mid-Atlantic in an airliner at 36,000 feet receiving a call on his mobile phone.

Again... no. Not then, anyway. He'd lost me well before that point for other reasons, but I can't stomach his writing anyway.

Don't assume you know anything. It is always best to double-check and the advent of the internet has made research a relatively simple task.

If you place a scene in a city that you don't know, get to a map, read the city's travel brochures, study pictures, read its history and become as familiar with the place as you can. If you want to mention a particular location as a place where somebody lives, make sure that it's not a city office location, or an industrial region with nothing but smoky factories and check that the socio-economic status matches the style of the person. Placing a multi-millionaire in his home in a slum region will cause you to lose one or more readers and damage your reputation.

If your hero must fly from London to Karachi, study the flight schedules, make sure the airline you name (and you *should* name it, that provides extra accuracy and reality to the tale) does actually fly that route and that it doesn't mean a change of flight and/or airline in perhaps Zurich or Copenhagen or Istanbul. Check what sort of aircraft is assigned to that route, don't assume it's a Boeing 747 or Airbus

380 or anything else. Check it, the airline website will almost certainly tell you, and if it doesn't, one of the international travel agency web sites will. These days, you can plan an entire itinerary on the internet, getting all times, flight durations, aircraft types, etc., listed for you.

I also recommend that you check the customs and immigration regulations for any foreign country that is a destination for your hero or villain. Some countries require visas, some don't, some nationalities are exempt from visa requirements in some countries. All these facts are normally available in the travel guides or the countries' own information websites.

Get your currencies correct. Don't have a bill in rupees when the action is in Bolivia. Look it up, check exchange rates and if values are mentioned, make sure they are realistic. Don't have somebody buying a $1000 item and paying the equivalent of $5 because you haven't got the currencies straight.

If the protagonist must drive from Venice to Paris, get to a map, get references from travel sites and make sure you know what routes are viable and how long it will take. If the trip starts at noon and ends at 3pm on the same day, you've got it horribly wrong and lots of people will know it.

If somebody is to fly into a foreign city and rent a car, find out what rental agencies operate from that airport and what sort of vehicles they provide. Go to their website, obtain a quote; it's easy providing you don't complete the transaction and pay for a reservation on your credit card. Again, get the map and check the route into the city. And read up about the car that is selected. Be sure of its size, performance, seating capacity and so on. Don't have four people travelling in a Ferrari two-seater, or have them load several suitcases into the trunk. They can't. If somebody is staying at a reputable hotel, check its website also, hopefully see some pictures of rooms, dining areas, public areas, views from suites, etc. It all helps the reality quotient.

And if you are going to talk murder, assassination and suchlike, it's even more important to get your facts straight. If shooting is involved, make sure that your character doesn't use a silencer, for example, if the gun is not actually made for one. And be careful here – silencers don't really work on an automatic pistol because the biggest noise is the supersonic crack the bullet makes. They don't work at all on a revolver because there is too much open space to be covered. To use a silencer effectively, the bullets must be chambered for subsonic travel. Don't, as one writer did once, have the hero detect the sound of the incoming rifle bullet – it's also supersonic and if he'd heard the bullet, it would already be past him (or in him if he survived the hit). Check the sort of calibres that might be used in revolvers, automatic pistols, rifles, etc. If somebody is using an automatic pistol, look up how many bullets can be stored in the magazine (it varies a lot) and don't have him shoot 15 rounds from a weapon that only carries six. And don't confuse a revolver with an automatic.

Poisons are another field where great care is essential. There are several guidebooks on this subject written specifically for writers of thrillers and crime dramas. If you can't get the information on the internet, which is unlikely, head for the bookshops or the booksellers' websites.

Another area where one can show one's amateurism is in names and accents of different nationalities. Names are not difficult, any telephone website can help there, though one of my favourite and treasured tools is the international directory of one of those humungous accounting firms that have offices in almost every country. I go through the offices listed for the country I have chosen for the character, pick a first name from one office, a second name from another and bingo. I have a valid and not stereotypical name.

And if including a foreign national in your story, go to the map, study the country's regions, determine where the character came from and read up about it, as there may be interesting facts about regional accents, dialects, cultures and so on. You can add extra colour, for example if your Polish woman actually speaks German as a first language, because in the far south of Poland that can happen, as in my mother's case. A Swiss might speak French or German or Italian, depending on his origins, or possibly all three, but select the appropriate characteristics. Check for dialects – a German might speak the *Hochdeutsch* (High German) of the north, or *Schweitzerdeutsch* (Swiss German). Chinese is worse. The Chinese citizens of Malaysia, Hong Kong and some others speak Cantonese, those of Singapore and mainland China speak Mandarin and some other dialects in different regions, such as Hokkien. It's a minefield there and needs careful research. Meanwhile, you'll be learning some fascinating stuff.

And don't have a German letting out *"Ach, so!"* or *"Mein Gott in Himmel!"* while otherwise speaking good English, nor have a Frenchman using an intermittent *"Mon Dieu!"* or *"Mon ami."* Leave that to Hercule Poirot. It makes the writer sound puerile. If a foreigner is speaking English well enough to have dialogue in your book, he is going to speak English and not lapse into other tongues.

If you use equipment, make sure that what you describe is accurate and current – go to the websites for the manufacturer, or "google" the topic and make sure everything is right. Computer technology is another minefield, given the speed of technological development. Don't let the company using a computer have one that vanished from the scene five or ten years ago, just because that's what you remember from a job you once held. Don't let the operations be obsolete, such as programmers writing in Cobol (yes I know, Cobol does still exist, but only very rarely is it used and not for new systems development). If you want to use that reference for specific purposes, make sure you make it clear that the programmers are modifying an ancient legacy system, or something similar. Don't have people using floppy discs or long-dead software packages like Wordstar or Visicalc. Don't show yourself to be out of date.

To sum up – research until you're weary of it. Hey, nobody said writing a novel was all creative glow, fun and fortune-making. It's damned hard work and you are most unlikely ever to make a dollar from it, but if you *have* to write, this is what is required of you. Check, double-check and check again until you are as certain as you possible can be that you have your story based on facts and reality. One slip can lose your readers and they are desperately hard to get in the first place.

Punctuation and Dialogue

One more way of losing your readers.

I publish a lot of books for other writers, which means intensive editing to get the books in shape and technically correct. It's a sad fact that few people know how to write dialogue and punctuate it correctly, so here is one more lecture that may save your book from immediate rejection.

Here are some right ways and wrong ways of writing dialogue.

Example 1

"My word," said Peter. "His lordship won't like that."
"What I'm thinking," said Peter, "is that his lordship won't like that."

The difference being that the first one is composed of two separate statements. *'My word'* is complete in itself and so the second part begins after a full stop and with a capital letter. The second example is one continuous statement broken by the *'said Peter'* phrase and thus continues after a comma and without an upper case first letter.

Example 2

Peter entered the room and said, "My word, his lordship won't like that."

Note - a comma after the 'said' but the quoted speech still begins with an upper case letter.

When to start a new paragraph

The two men walked into the room.

"My word," said Peter. "His lordship won't like that."

BUT

Peter entered the room. "My word," he said. "His lordship won't like that."

i.e., if the speech is uttered by the character being referenced, it can continue in the same paragraph. But it is also correct to start a new paragraph with the quoted speech.

SO

Peter entered the room.

"My word," he said. "His lordship won't like that."
is also correct.

In fact, providing the paragraph continues to reference a single character, the quotations can remain within the same paragraph. Thus:

Peter entered the room. "My word," he said. "His lordship won't like that." He studied the drinks cabinet.

"He sent me down for Laphroaig scotch and all we have is gin." He looked round the room. "Who drank all the Laphroaig?" he asked.

But if more than one person is speaking in a conversation or discussion, each new speaker gets a new paragraph.

This is **INCORRECT**:

"Drat," Peter said. "His lordship won't like that." "Why not?" asked Samantha. "He wants scotch, not gin," said Peter.

This is **CORRECT**:

"Drat," Peter said. "His lordship won't like that."
"Why not?" asked Samantha.
"Because he wants scotch, not gin," said Peter.

NOTE:

"Because he wants scotch, not gin," said Peter.

"Because he wants scotch, not gin!" said Peter.

In both cases, 'said' is written with a lower case first character even though the exclamation point (or question mark) normally signifies the end of a sentence, equivalent to a full stop.

ALSO:

"Because he wants scotch, not gin," said Peter.

"Because he wants scotch, not gin," Peter said.

Both are correct and are simply the preference of the writer.

ALSO

Correct:

"Because he wants scotch, not gin," said Peter.

Incorrect:

"Because he wants scotch, not gin" said Peter.

"Because he wants scotch, not gin", said Peter.

"Because he wants scotch, not gin." said Peter.

"Because he wants scotch, not gin".

"Because he wants scotch, not gin"!

Chapter 13 – Actually Writing the Book

Alright, so you have brainstormed though many hours, probably over a period of some months and derived the major storyline for your novel. Many times, I am sure, you will have that dreaded "Writers' Block" when you have absolutely no idea how to proceed, how to get out of the logical pit you have dug for yourself or how to wind up the whole thing.

The brainstorming group will get you going again, count on it. Remember, this is not a book about creative writing. This is a book designed to generate ideas and overcome every roadblock, from getting started to finishing off. How often you need your group will depend on your time, your progress, the group members' time and how complex a book you are writing. But a reasonable estimate is perhaps three or four weekly meetings to generate the skeleton for perhaps a half of the book. Then a month or two of grinding hard work as you actually write the story as far as you can. Then another couple of sessions, possibly on consecutive days, followed by another few weeks of writing. After that, it's up to you and your style, your skill and your work ethic.

Now and again, you will run into a difficulty that you don't feel merits a full brainstorming session. There are two ways of resolving this that I have found to work over the years. Again, just like this whole methodology, they come from a previous incarnation, this time as a mediocre computer programmer writing programs in Cobol.

The technique my more senior and capable colleagues recommended was simply to discuss the problem with somebody, whether they knew about the system or not. They may never actually say a word, but in the process of describing the problem to them, you will see the solution. Countless times when I had a bug in my Cobol program that I simply couldn't see, I did as suggested, take aside the most junior programmer available, follow the code on the print-out and describe the bug and what was happening. Most times I had the problem resolved before the other person had even thought about the issue.

The other approach takes more courage. Give the manuscript to somebody you trust and ask them to read it. I have previously described this process as akin to running naked down the High Street and it really is. But in the process of giving your work to somebody else, somehow you will go back to it and read it again as if through somebody else's eyes and you will get a whole new perspective on it.

One more tip. Do not preach to the reader, unless that is the point of your book. If you have written a thriller or detective novel, avoid the trap of preaching some sort of message when it has absolutely nothing to do with the story. I fell badly into that trap with *"Dreamkill,"* my first published novel when I couldn't help but spout morally about computer operations from the standpoint of my then professional status as a business consultant. Thankfully, when the rights were returned to me, I deleted all that crud and republished a much cleaner book.

There was a period when I was debating the issue of guns with some Americans who were firmly convinced that an armed citizenry could defeat a tyranny and for their sake I read a couple of "Gunny" novels to see if they did, as claimed, clarify the issue. Most of the books seemed to consist of preaching enthusiastically that guns were the God-given rights of all men and that all men (and women) should carry a gun, or several guns at all times. Okay, but I wanted to see just how that would guarantee freedom from a tyranny and I never saw that anywhere. Both the works I read were intensely boring and irritating. They were written for believers and never questioned any of the standard dogma. They would never convert an unbeliever.

So don't preach.

Which leads to another point;

One of the standard truisms of the writing game is, *"Write about what you know."* It still holds true, but it can be overdone. Many writers have forced their story lines down a path in which they can now demonstrate just how much they know about a certain topic. I did it myself with my first (unpublished) effort, *"Corrupting Influences."* I knew two things well, computer consulting and flying sailplanes. I tried writing a book in which both topics were interwoven. It didn't work. The book remains on my computer and occasionally I bring it up on the screen and admire my splendid descriptions of flying sailplanes and shudder at how out of date are the computer sections. I fiddle with a few bits here and there and save it back into the file.

As I wrote the first edition of this work, I was reading a book by an Australian writer, an ex-priest. It's not a bad thriller with religious overtones, but at one point the writer decides to tell the reader what an expert he, the writer, is at climbing. So something has to be hidden in a secret place up a high cliff, and we are treated to detailed descriptions of equipment and techniques that may excite another climber but not me. I didn't finish the book. It's similar to preaching but with educational overtones.

Anyway, the advent of the internet makes the truism less of one. You can get to know about almost everything well enough to sound convincing if you know how to do research.

You have embarked on a frighteningly difficult, complex and time-consuming project that will exhaust you, sometimes bore you, educate you, often exhilarate you and hopefully fulfil you.

Let me offer one more thought that may help you. At some stage, maybe after you have finished the book or possibly before, there is every chance that you will decide the book is rubbish and you're never going to make it as a writer.

Here's a message of real hope. Some years ago, I found in a second-hand book shop in Chicago, a book bearing the name of one of my favourite authors, A Great Writer who had better remain nameless. I paid a whole quarter and took the book away to read in my hotel, settled down after dinner and opened the book.

Within a few pages I started laughing. This book was simply the *worst* novel I had ever read. It was excruciatingly bad. It had every cliché of every potboiler ever written. The plot was puerile, characters barely even two-dimensional, dialogue so stilted I couldn't read a sentence aloud without bursting out with laughter, every situation was predictable, especially the ending. It was mind-bogglingly, blood-curdlingly, spine-bendingly *awful*. I suddenly realised how inspirational this book was. Bad as my first (and second and third) novels had been, they were a *lot* better than this thing.

This appalling crud was something The Great Writer had obviously written as perhaps his very first effort at writing a novel and which had been deservedly laughed out of the literary agent's office, then dug up and published some years later after fame had arrived. But if the writer of this nonsense could eventually become The Great Writer, one of my favourites and a truly fine writer of international espionage and similar thrillers, then I could do it also and possibly better, as I had a head start.

I take this novel with me to the markets and show it to the writers and wannabe writers who come and talk to me and explain how I read this thing every now and again to reinforce my self-confidence.

Seriously, while your first novel may well be poor and unworthy of publication (as are most first novels), it is almost *bound* to be better than The Great Writer's early effort and thus gives you a head start also.

Okay, finish this book and then get down to what you really want to do – write your own book.

I can do no more than wish you the very best of luck and hope to see your book on the shelves one day.

Chapter 14 – Publishing and Selling Your Book

I have had only one book published by the conventional process. That was *"Dreamkill,"* my first-published work and my fifth novel to be written. This was while living in the USA and I submitted the book to 40 literary agents, all of whom rejected it with varying degrees of contempt. The 41st took it, made me rewrite it extensively, charging me a fortune in the process and did eventually sell it to a publisher in Utah (the 25th submission) who made a real pig's ear of publishing it, ignoring half the corrections I'd made on the galley proofs.

Soon after, they went bankrupt when the owners absconded with all the money in the corporate coffers and they may still be in prison for all I know or care. But the copyright was returned to me by the Utah State Supreme Court. I rewrote it extensively and self-published.

I tried submitting my other completed works in the USA, Canada and the UK and met absolute blank walls. My favourite reason for rejection by agents was with *"The Nightmares of God."* Several agents in Britain, Canada and the USA said they loved it, were utterly stunned by it and one thought it could become a cult novel along with the likes of *"Dune," "2001,"* *"Childhood's End"* and Asimov's *"Foundation"* series. But they said not a publisher in the US would touch it for fear of rousing the rage and reactions of the so-called "Religious Right" and so nobody else would either. I took that as high praise indeed and determined that one day I wanted to see the American Televangelists on the religious channels, waving my book while spitting fury and hate and declaring *"The Nightmares of God"* to be the work of Satan and must be banned and the writer killed. A Southern Baptist *Fatwah,* no less. I intend to send them some copies one day.

When I returned home to Australia, I tried again, thinking that perhaps having had one book published in the USA, literary agents and publishers would look more positively at me. I was soon cured of that delusion.

Here are the main problems with literary agents and publishers in Australia:

The average literary agent gets anything up to 2,000 unsolicited manuscripts a month into their offices.

Most of them are rubbish and go to the "Dreck Pile."

Even if the book is excellent, if it has not grabbed the agent's attention within five or six pages, it also goes to the Dreck Pile.

Now and again, some poor slob, usually a trainee or junior agent is assigned to dredging through the Dreck Pile in the hope they find something worthwhile.

Usually they don't, or can't see the merits of what they examine.

Most of the literary agents know little of any value about literature. You may well have heard of the exercises repeated every year or so all over the world of people retyping famous works of literature or highly successful works by great writers of a couple of decades ago and submitting them as originals to literary agents. Such works include Jane Austin, Thomas Keneally, Anthony Trollope and similar great writers who still outsell almost all other current writers.

Not only are these manuscripts rejected, but the agents clearly do not even recognise them for what they are.

This does not inspire faith.

But even if you manage to get your work avoid or be picked out of the Dreck Pile, the agent offers you representation and submits your work to an Australian publisher you will run into the second hurdle on the course.

I submitted *"The Many Worlds of Mickie Dalton"* to over thirty agents in Australia and one finally called me to offer representation. That was a huge thrill and when I told the kids at St. Josephs, they were delighted. We had established a goal for this project of beating the crap out of Harry Potter and we felt we were at last on the way.

But then as my agent submitted the book to Australian publishers, I hit that second obstacle.

They don't want you. Nor do the big distributors like Angus and Robinson and Dymocks. And one can understand why. While there may be an element of "cultural cringe" in place, the assumption that Australian writers can't be any good, mostly it's economic. The sales window for a book on the shelves is only a matter of a few weeks, after which the book is discarded and forgotten. First-time Australian writers don't get much interest from readers either. So the obvious business path for all concerned is to take only the few Australian and those overseas writers of established reputations and sell those. The corporations cannot make money from first-time Australian writers.

My Masters' Degree in Business Administration applauds this as sound business policy. Under my Australian writer's hat (an Akubra, of course), I rage at the refusal to acknowledge a responsibility to encourage local talent, of which there is a huge well of very great ability indeed.

Now I appreciate that all the above sounds like the whining of almost every author under the sun. And almost every author under the sun can tell similar tales of submissions to many, many agents and publishers and building a collection a metre thick of rejection slips. They are all true.

These include highly successful writers like John Marsden who I believe sold books from the boot of his car for some time before his talents were finally recognised.

My recommendation – don't go that route. It's bad for the ego, wastes postage and a great deal of time, stretches the nerves and generally is a total waste of energy.

But by all means, try it if you wish. You never know, you might be the one in several million people each year who can get a new book published. I actually met one of those in Nambucca Heads. She came to my presentation at a Writers' Open Day at Nambucca Heads Library and bless her! she didn't sneer at me. But she didn't really know why her book had been selected for publication and so many others never made it past the Dreck Pile.

So give it a go. But don't let it interfere with your self-publishing project, because you can get three books written and published in the time it will take to find a literary agent, for him or her to see the merit of your worth, submit it to a publisher and have them make you an offer, have it edited to *their* (not your) satisfaction and then finally print it and start distribution.

The time between acceptance and seeing your book in your hand can be several years. "*Mickie Dalton*" had actually been the subject of interest with one publisher for three years without a decision being made and my agent said that the modern approach was to submit to only one publisher at a time until a decision was made.

There's another problem! You may not actually want the fruits of success that come from a publisher's adopting your book and making you The Next Big Thing In Literature. It can be very dangerous to your health.

Some time ago I was watching a program on television in which four famous, very successful writers were discussing this issue with the host. Not one of them seemed happy with their success. They had lost control of their books to the publisher who made changes to *their* standards, not those of the writer; they had lost control of their own lives by having to produce on demand and appear at author's signing days to a schedule set by the publisher; and they had no say in cover design which had been passed to the marketing people who set a "brand" design common to all the writer's books.

One even seemed to indicate that he wished the success had never happened.

So take the increasingly popular path of huge numbers of writers and self-publish your work.

There are a number of serious advantages to this path:

First, you guarantee that you will see your published work and hold it in your hands, see it on your bookshelf and show it to friends and family. For the greatest majority of us, that is sufficient. It is the consummation of many years of dreaming and work, especially if it is an autobiography written for the sake of one's descendents.

Second, you keep control of your work. If a publisher takes your work, he *takes* it; copyright, movie rights, the lot, unless you get a savvy lawyer onto the task. And should your book be sold through the usual distribution channels, you the writer receive 15% of the retail price, from which you pay at least 10% to your agent. All this for perhaps 500 or so copies sold. It's not worth it. I sold more than that of most of my published works in the first 18 months of serious marketing and I make about $7-12 gross profit on each, more in the case of my biggest book, *"The Nightmares of God."*

Third, you can ensure that your book will be read by at least *some* people by donating them to local libraries. Almost all libraries will be delighted to receive the works of local writers – they are about the only organisations that do understand their responsibilities to nurture local talent. And they will be happy to report loan statistics to you. I have been given the cold shoulder by only one library so far and it still baffles me why they would reject free books.

The downside of all this, of course is that your books won't move unless you do the work.

Self publishing is becoming easier and easier. As the demand for "Print on Demand" services has grown, the supply of organisations offering the service has increased and costs have gone down. My initial research for printers of the Mickie Dalton trilogy led me to have the works printed in the USA. Since then, local organisations have increased in number and the Australian dollar has changed in value and it is quite economic to have your books printed in Australia. Some writers now tell me they get their works published in China at far lower cost than I give below, but then one also faces delays, transportation times and costs, import duties, slow reaction times and potentially hazardous language issues. I still prefer to publish my books in Australia.

An average 300-page book will cost you about $15 a copy, far less if you have large runs produced, and I sell these for between $20-25 each. My biggest work *"The Nightmares of God"* (648 pages) costs me about $19 each, including GST and postage and I sell it for $35. These costs are for A5 size, black and white content only, no colour within the body of the book, paperback glossy covers in colour. Go to the internet, research printers and get competitive quotes.

The printers will produce exactly what you send them, no more, no less. That produces two issues; one is to get your work proof-read and preferably edited also. That means some up-front costs but they are definitely worth it. I do most strongly recommend having your book read by a professional proof-reader. You will reach a point after some weeks of working on your book where you simply cannot see the typos and similar errors. The second issue is cover-design and creation and also ISBN numbers and bar codes.

Your printer will help you arrange ISBN numbers, or you can contact Thorpe-Bowker in Melbourne, (www.thorpe.com.au) the organisation which controls these numbers. If you buy only a single number, you pay about $65 and then a similar amount for a barcode. If you buy a batch of ten, as I do, the numbers come out at $8 each. And a decent software package for cover design is also essential, but pays for itself many times over if you write subsequent books, especially as the software will generate the bar codes for you, merely by entering the ISBN Number. For this, I use "Book Cover Pro" which cost me about $200 (the price can vary) but with more than fifty books done so far, either for me ort for clients, this has more than paid for itself. But if you want a designer to develop the artwork, be prepared to pay for that service. So far, I have done my own, using artwork I can download for free from the internet or merely simple layouts, but I have had to upgrade this process as I become more established and sales increase. I learned to use "Photoshop" which has given me greater flexibility in creating cover designs and also for illustrations in the children's books I write with school children.

The process from then on is then quite simple:

- Write your book using the brainstorming techniques and guidance from this work;
- Get it proofread and edited;
- Get your ISBN number; and
- Design your cover.

Look at other books in the same genre for some indicators as to font size, layouts, the un-numbered and un-headed pages for dedications, statements as to copyright and so on and lay out the entire book to your satisfaction. If necessary, get some professional advice as to fonts, sizes, headers, etc.

Produce your work in PDF format. That's easy, most office software includes a PDF conversion routine. You may also need a software package that will produce JPG format images from any work you produce, if you want to create images for the cover. These are cheap enough, certainly under $100 and can be downloaded through the internet.

When you have had your quotes, submit the work to your selected publisher.

You will probably be offered a single proof copy first, for about $100, which covers set-up and other costs. Study it line by line, because sometimes errors occur in the conversion from your PDF to the printer's software. I found several such errors and had to get them cleaned up by the printer first.

Once you are happy with the work, order as many copies as you want. Most organisations will offer any number of copies, from one to as many as you choose.

Naturally, the unit cost per book goes down as the size of the print run increases.

But the printer produces exactly what you send them. That does present a problem. It's like the old computer programming mantra, GIRO - "Garbage In, Rubbish Out." If you have written rubbish, it remains rubbish. So I do recommend strongly that you have a professional editor look over your work and advise just how viable is your book. At least make sure that your grammar, spelling and writing are of an acceptable standard and there is some sort of flow there.

I looked at one manuscript some while ago which was really written as a manifesto for the writer's special passion. (Remember – don't preach.) It was a pretty awful novel anyway, but he had packed it out by incorporating large chunks of writing from his academic work on the subject, including bullet points and technical writing techniques. That made it quite dreadful and not remotely suitable for publishing. It needed serious re-writing, so even though the message was worth pushing, that book would never achieve it. Fiction and technical writing styles do not mix.

So be sure you are submitting something that does actually merit printing.

The self-publishing route is the path I finally chose mainly because the kids at St. Josephs had reached their final year and I was not going to let them graduate without seeing the results of their work. I just made it, getting them their three books on the final school assembly of their year and it made the whole thing worthwhile.

But then I realised that it was not a hugely expensive process after all and I decided to do the same with the other four books that I had completed and considered worth reading, leaving five others that are still worthy only of the Dreck Pile.

Seeing *"Dreamkill"* in print back in 1996 had been an enormous thrill. Seeing the Mickie Dalton Trilogy was no less a thrill, and getting *"The Nightmares of God"* was pretty exciting also, as many of my friends had said it was really a great book. Soon after, I had all seven books in print and I spent a considerable amount of time simply admiring them on my bookshelves. One of them was the revised and updated *"Dreamkill."*

So I began marketing. It needed a website and that was done. I donated copies of all seven books to several local library systems and was delighted to find that people did actually borrow them. I approached two local bookshops and they agreed to take them on consignment. I approached the local newspaper and had a pretty good, full-page article published.

I started a market stall at the local market and then at several other markets. Now I do one every Sunday and two Saturdays a month. The Mickie Dalton Trilogy gave me an opening with schools. Several teachers or school librarians talked to me at markets and bought the trilogy, in return for which I offered to run writing workshops with their English students, or just talk to the students about the writing game, and I have done several of these events. I started a wonderful new project much like the one at St Josephs High School, but this time with a primary school and each week I met with ten little ones aged 8-10 as we developed a complete children's adventure story using this brainstorming technique. Just as before, the kids blew me away with their imagination and enthusiasm and a seriously good story developed, involving international smuggling of Australian native species, something that is a major problem. *"The Julie Malloy Gang and the Smugglers"* was published in December, 2009.

Following that, I did two more projects with small primary schools with the same results. The schools were close together, so I met with one group at 9am on a Thursday and the second group at 11am. I offered each group a range of initial premises and each picked a different one, though several parallels developed between the two, both books involving connections to the Romanov Family that once ruled Russia until the revolution of 1917. So the project became an invaluable teaching exercise as well and the children were fascinated by the history. Both *"The Quest for the Locket"* and *"The Secret of Yuri Kirilenko"* were published in June, 2010.

A profound discovery during these projects was the groups aged between seven and twelve produced stories involving international espionage that would have been considered suitable for the 15-17 age group. Some of the kids also read *"The Mickie Dalton Trilogy"* aimed at the 12-18 age group. All of this tells me that we seriously underestimate the kids' intellects and abilities and this is to be the topic of a conversation to be held with the educational authorities.

I talk to groups like Rotary and have conducted several presentations at libraries in the region.

At my market stall, I have long, wonderful conversations with teachers, librarians, writers, wannabe writers, other self-published writers and others. Most writers have the same horror stories of blank rejections by publishers and agents. Those who have published their works get my offer to display their books on my stall. I have ten other writers now and have doubled the table space.

Usually, I sell a few books, mine and theirs.

Along the way, something odd has happened. I don't understand how this happened or when it happened, but happen it did. I stopped being that daft old bloke trying to sell his books at the market and became a writer. Other writers asked me to review their manuscripts and I will always do that. Some have been astonishing. At least one I believe is best-seller material and I have begged the writer to get it proofread and edited and then published. I'll display it, but I firmly believe she's up there with the best and it will make its own way to fame.

Another one had great potential as a medieval thriller, but her style verged dangerously on the Harlequin Romance level. I made some suggestions, she rewrote the offending chapters and now I think she's another one with best-seller potential.

Now I get calls to be the keynote speaker at various functions. I get other calls from readers who just want to tell me how much they enjoyed one of my books, either borrowed from the library or bought at a market. Another interesting sales opening is growing with several agents who will create catalogues with self-published writers' works and conduct marketing through corporations, reader parties, book fairs, etc.

So life is at a very exciting stage. If nothing else, I take huge delight in knowing that not only have I written one complete and readable novel, I have now completed twenty-three plus this textbook. Selling every book at market is a wildly exciting moment because somebody has deemed a book of mine worth paying out money for it and will go away and actually read it. There was once a time when I was worried, concerned that they'd be back telling me it was rubbish, but I have never experienced anything but highly positive comments. The delight of that never fails, regardless of how often it happens.

Every single one of you can do the same, it just takes time and persistence. I believe that if you follow the methodology of this book, you can at least cut the time required to write that first novel and, like every other form of exercise, the more you do, the easier and better it gets.

Don't seriously expect your first book to go the way of *"Harry Potter"* or *"The da Vinci Code."* Expect to be like the rest of us mortals and decide that the book is really not that great at all. But the second, or the third or any subsequent one may well be the one that changes your life.

So call your group together, get the whiteboard up, get the pens, start brainstorming. You may be surprised at how rapidly you complete your novel and see if published and in your hands. Even if you never sell a copy beyond a few to friends and family, you can be immensely proud of the fact that you have achieved something that millions of people dream about doing and never get there.

Now – *GET TO WORK!!!*

Samples of Some Other Works by Michael Davies

The Mickie Dalton Trilogy – A Science-Fiction Adventure for Young Adults aged 12-17

Chapter 1 – A Miserable Home

Twelve-year old Mickie Dalton looked round the dining table and knew he had to leave home.

His father was crouched over the newspaper like a vulture examining a corpse, slurping his soup and intermittently erupting with a snort like a diesel engine threatening to draw the oxygen from the room. When he reached for a slice of bread, he bit into it then jammed the remainder into his mouth as if the bread might struggle and slip away. The smacking sound of his eating was even noisier than the soup-slurping. Mickie's mother had put down her spoon and was surreptitiously eyeing her packet of Player's Extra Mild cigarettes, parked with its box of matches dangerously close to her right hand. The ashtray, a handbreadth farther away, already contained two lipstick-tipped stubs of earlier satisfaction. Mickie prayed that she wouldn't succumb to the temptation, for, if she did, smoke and ash would float over the table again, settling on his food and giving it an acrid, bitter taste. His father would follow the example, making the air even worse, while his mother's hacking cough would blast through the room before she spat phlegm into her handkerchief. Sometimes, Mickie gagged and nearly threw up when she did that, which invariably got his father's attention, which was always a dangerous thing.

"Please, God, don't let her take a cigarette," pleaded Mickie silently but with little hope. "Please don't let her start coughing and spitting. Please don't make him take one, as well. Please, God."

Apparently immune to the noisy proceedings and his desperate communion with the Supreme Deity, Mickie's older sister, an incomprehensibly alien creature separated from him by exactly two years, stared blankly at the centre of the table. Mickie had no idea where her mind was. She picked her nose idly, a crime tolerated in her, but punishable by a furious thrashing if committed by him.

Mickie disliked them all intensely. He knew he could leave home at sixteen. He knew that, because he had asked his teacher at school what was the earliest time he could go off and start work. She seemed upset by the question, for reasons that Mickie could not understand, but told him the answer gently. Once again in an endless series of times, he tried to comprehend the idea of four more years of this terrifying, damaging and miserable place called his home. *Four more years.* That was about a third as long again as he had lived already. It was a time-scale by which to measure the lives of stars and galaxies. He had no idea how to survive it.

His father sniffed again, and the ugly noise gave his mother permission for her urgent want and need to be satisfied. She reached hungrily for the cigarette packet, almost tearing the cardboard as she opened it. Mickie knew that the second course would be delayed by another fifteen minutes and would taste awful when it came.

The smoke hit him, and he coughed. He struggled for breath and coughed again. His father lowered the paper and glared at him.

"What's the matter with you?" he snapped.

Mickie felt panic wash over his body like slimy water. His throat constricted, his cheeks flamed. To the side, he saw his sister return to the world, and stare at him in the same furious way as his father as if trying to share the rage and enjoy it more. Anticipation grew in her eyes. Mickie stared down at his plate, paralysed by the familiar, awful events unfolding.

"Nothing," he mumbled.

"What do you mean, nothing?" shouted his father. He crushed the paper under his arms, warming up for action. Paralysing terror overtook Mickie. He could only shake his head.

"I said, what do you *MEAN*? Eh? What do you mean?" The shout had become a roar. The man stood up, threw the paper to one side and grabbed Mickie by the shoulder.

"Look!" he bellowed, bending over the boy. "I'm totally fed up with you, you stupid little pig!" His right hand landed flat and hard on Mickie's cheek, and Mickie fell backward against his chair. Familiar terror ran through him mixed with shame and anger that he had to put up with this senseless and undeserved violence once more.

"Oh, Jack, he didn't mean anything." At last, his mother spoke. She didn't seem all that worried. Her cigarette was lit and in its place in the corner of her mouth, and all was right with her world. Her husband ignored her. Another open-handed slap landed on Mickie's cheek, rocking him sideways. He could barely breathe and could look nowhere but down at the floor as the violence flared around him. His cheeks stung and the heat of his shame made the tears feel cold as they ran.

"Now get upstairs to your room!" said his father in cold contempt, his anger for the moment sated by the short burst of violence.

Struggling to keep the tears away and losing, Mickie ran out of the room, up the stairs and into his tiny bedroom. He resisted the urge to slam the door behind, because nothing was more certain to bring his father roaring into his room to administer another beating. He sat on his bed, the tears falling freely down his face. He was hungry, but he knew he would not see anything of the meal tonight. His mother had more important things to concern her than bringing him dinner.

Apart from his single bed the bare, stark room contained nothing but, a simple kitchen chair and a small table where he did his homework. There was a book lying on the table. He stood, picked up the book and pushed the chair to the open window. There would be enough light to read for another hour or two on this English summer night. Then he would have to retreat into imagination of a different sort, for electric light was not permitted in his room. He still had bruises from the last time his father had seen the dim glow of the small bulb, thundered into his room and kicked him out of bed shouting, "Who the hell pays the electricity bill around here?" Mickie wondered why both parents and his sister were able to read in their rooms without that unanswerable query being raised. It was merely another element of the great mystery of why his father hated him so much.

Downstairs, both parents erupted into coughing fits that inexorably followed the lighting of a new cigarette. Mickie rubbed his eyes, wiped his nose, and opened the book. Within minutes, he was lost in the thunderous, bloody story of *Beowulf*.

When it became too dark to read any further, he crawled into bed. In the friendly gloom he imagined scenes of great excitement and action with himself as the hero. He flew jet fighters, defeated vicious killers with breathtaking displays of swordsmanship then stared with contempt at his father whom he had just rescued from painful death. Murderous beasts roared into the streets of the Manchester suburb and were destroyed by the astounding weapons he'd invented, leaving him to bask in the adoring gaze of the girls from his classroom. He developed brilliant conversations with his sister, defeated her every argument she could raise against him, killed her every statement with intellect and brilliance until she was left downcast, crest-fallen and embarrassed, acknowledging her brother's superiority with a bad grace.

At one point, he heard his father erupt into a monstrous coughing fit. A wave of anger swept over him. How *dare* that man spend so much on cigarettes while leaving his son with threadbare clothes? The rage seemed to rise to a peak and he felt an odd sensation as if he had sneezed within his head but not through his nose. The coughing fit downstairs changed into a cry of pain and fear. He heard his mother shriek "Jack! What's the matter?" The bangs of furniture being knocked about echoed through the house and then the racket subsided.

Puzzled, but unable to avoid feeling a sense of satisfaction at the man's distress, Mickie relaxed again.

As he drifted into that limbo state between wakefulness and sleep, his imagination ran riot. He heard a strange, powerful, yet immensely distant and invisible voice that seemed to be shouting something familiar. He saw images of tiny, beautiful people who led him by the hand through pathways in dense cities of trees and laughed with limitless joy at the wonders of their world. An imposing being with a head like a wild boar stood before him and bellowed in friendly welcome, one impossibly huge right arm draped under a cloak, while on the left, two smaller arms looked delicate in comparison. A child stood by his parents and they smiled at Mickie, and they had blue faces, reddish hair and no nose at all, but he felt a wave of friendship from them. And just as he fell asleep, a wonderfully warm, gentle voice, he was sure it was a woman, spoke to him with love and comfort. Despite the awful evening in a series of awful evenings, for those few moments Mickie felt happier than he had ever been before.

When he woke up, both parents were coughing in desperation, having just lit the first cigarettes of the day.

Mickie didn't know it, but he wouldn't have to wait four years before leaving home. He had only two days left on Earth.

The Nightmares of God – A Sci-Fi novel about the end of the Universe and its rebirth

Chapter 1. The First Tendril

The end of all of Time and Creation began early in the 21st Century, but nobody on Earth knew it at the time. Despite their initial ignorance of the enormity of what was happening, several individuals played significant roles in bringing about the final chapter of the story of Creation.

(From the diary of Father Alan Drew, discovered in 2067 in a cottage in Maine, in the Canadian Province of Arcadia, where he is believed to have spent his last years.)
April 9, 2012

The old man frightens me. He's dead now, and I watched him die, but still he frightens me. Perhaps he was right, and the world is coming to an end. Perhaps an old drunk dying in an alleyway has seen the Day of Judgement coming.

He was staggering, reeling against the walls of the seedy suburb when I saw him. I walked out of the church where I had just given the evening service, and the man was but a few yards away. I moved to him, just as he collapsed, banging his face against the red brick wall of the deserted factory. I rushed to his huddled form, and turned him on his back, recoiling as a wave of evil breath reached me. I forgot the distaste in the awful fact that the man was dying.

His eyes seemed focused on some infinitely distant event. Pale drool ran from the corner of his mouth and down his cheek. I took off my jacket and folded it on the hard concrete, then lifted his head and rested it on the makeshift pillow. I saw his eyes withdraw from infinity and touch briefly on my collar, then on my face.

"Oh, father," he said in an unexpectedly soft voice. The accent was North Country, Yorkshire, I thought, not the local Nottingham tones. "Strange that I should be telling a priest."

"Telling me what, my son?" I asked, pulling my bag toward me and reaching for the phone.

"It's all over," he said and smiled. His eyes moved to the phone in my hand. "There's no point in that, father," he said. "And I wouldn't want to hang around anyway. Not any more."

"Life is God's gift, my son," I replied. "It is not ours to throw away, even if Heaven awaits us." I pushed the emergency buttons on the phone.

"Heaven?" The old man tried to laugh, and nearly choked. "There's no Heaven, father! Nor a Hell, either. I just saw that."

"I don't want you to find out for a long time yet," I said as firmly as I could, knowing that the man's death was minutes away. I spoke into the tiny telephone as a voice answered, and I gave directions.

"But I have found out," he replied, and smiled at me with such love and happiness that my heart seemed to stop. "It's all over, father. You can throw that dog collar away. It's coming."

"What's coming, my son?" I didn't understand his words, but I felt a tendril of some incomprehensibly vast power touch my soul.

His eyes moved outward again. The expression on his face was a mixture of awe and happiness. He clutched my arm, though he seemed unaware of his act.

"Oh, it's so beautiful," he whispered. "I never dreamed it could be so beautiful."

I was certain now that his last moments had come. I had heard of people in their last seconds of life seeing tunnels leading to wonderful light and happiness.

"Are you seeing the tunnel to heaven, my son?" I asked, reaching back into my bag for the purple sash and other materials I knew I would need in seconds. His eyes turned back to me, and they suddenly shone with caring, as if our positions were reversed.

"It's not a tunnel, father. It's Oneness."

"What?" I asked, feeling my voice tremble without knowing why.

But he was dead.

I put the sash round my neck, and opened the tiny vial of holy water. The small sounds of a siren provided a backdrop to the words I began to speak.

The conversation in that dirty alleyway remained with me till late that night. I prayed for the soul of the old drunk and tried not to think about what he meant by "Oneness." By the next morning, I had returned again to the excitement of the news I had received the previous week. I am to be seconded to the Holy City. I will work with His Holiness for the next two years. That such an honour would come to me at the age of just thirty is far beyond my expectations and more than I deserve, but I will work my hardest to represent my Bishop in the Vatican. But to see Pope Jean-Pierre II every day. I am surely blessed.

But I cannot shake that conversation from my mind. "Oneness?" What in our Lord's heaven could he have meant?

The Janus Conspiracy

Prologue - Berlin, April 30th, 1945

It was the city's last day.

Not a building stood whole. Bodies lay in the streets like broken dolls after a demonic children's party. Some of the bodies wore the uniform of the Red Army, but most of them were in the dark field-grey of German troops. Many were corpses of children, women, old people who had watched the Soviet army units of General Zhukov drive through the last defences of Berlin like a White Pointer shark attacking a wounded swimmer. The sharp stink of explosives mixed with the burning smell of charred flesh, pulverized stone and the stench of fear.

Dmitri Alexandrovitch was pale, his eyes black and haunted. No combat in the clean air, however filled with blind terror as aircraft flung themselves at each other like rabid hawks, nothing had prepared him for the death of a civilization.

"This is a vision of Hell, Yuri," Dmitri said into a small gap in the sounds of dying.

"This, Dmitri? Hell? It's just the antechamber. We have seen worse." Yuri's smile was cold. He would be twenty-three in four months, but his face was that of some ancient mystic in a painting by a Dutch master. A thousand years of pain burned in the blue eyes of his fine, aristocratic features.

The two brothers stood apart from the steady file of Russian soldiers walking along the rubble of what had been a broad, graceful street. The faces under the helmets of the infantrymen were no longer human. Too much death, too much killing, starvation and pitiless destruction had removed their souls. The men were now machines made of perishable and destructive material, quickened only by a lust to kill anything that was not one of their own. Ten minutes earlier, Dmitri had watched a trio of men bayonet a woman and her three children. There had been no joy in the savagery. It had been automatic, brutal killing on the way to the centre of the evil they had come to destroy. The *Fuehrerbunker*, the last refuge of Adolph Hitler lay only a few hundred metres ahead, and they wanted to be at the kill.

"Perhaps," Dmitri said. "We have both seen horrors. We have seen the best of our young men die. We have seen our

9

Mother Russia battered to a pulp as that lunatic Georgian worked his insane fantasies on her, killing thousands if he felt that a man's eyes had looked at him wrongly. There is no hell like seeing one's own history and culture destroyed by a megalomaniac."

Yuri smiled without humour. "There was a time, dear elder brother, when you almost bowed when you heard the name of Joseph Stalin. The Great Father, we called him, the bearer of the mantle of Lenin himself, saviour of all Russia."

"He killed our dreams, together with the millions of kulaks, the workers, the intelligentsia and the best officers of our army and navy." Dmitri watched another file of men pick their way through the rubble. "He betrayed the Revolution. We survived the Romanovs and the Mensheviks, and for what? To have another Tsar, ten times more bloodthirsty even than Ivan the Terrible or the hideous Catherine?"

"Why did you come here, big brother?" Yuri asked. "And in the uniform of a Colonel in General Katukov's First Guards? I tell you, it was a major shock to see you this morning, striding into the camp as if you had been an infantryman all your life."

For the first time, Dmitri smiled. "Instead of flying like an eagle above all this horror? Why, to save you, little one. I could no longer leave my baby brother to face the dangers of this war without the protection of his older, and so much wiser sibling."

"A true brother," Yuri said, smiling back. "I am, of course, pathetically grateful for your protection, oh ancient one of such wisdom, but what is the real reason?"

A shell crashed into the walls of an already shattered building a few hundred yards away, and the remaining walls collapsed, the noise of the fall lost in the turmoil. Yuri pulled his brother inside the doorway of the church near which they had been standing.

"You still believe in the Revolution, little brother?" Dmitri asked, slapping dust and grime from his uniform.

"Dmitri! You want to discuss political philosophy at this place and time? We might be dead at any moment. And anyway, I want to be with my men as we catch that madman, Adolph Hitler. He is probably within two hundred metres of us right now."

"I'm deadly serious, Yuri." Dmitri looked deeply into his

brother's eyes. "Is your heart and soul still with the dreams of Lenin and Marx, that only through communism can we achieve world peace and fairness?"

Yuri stared at his brother. The deadly, intense seriousness of the other man's face and words rang through the death throes of the Third Reich proceeding with such slaughter and destruction around them. "Yes, Dmitri," he replied finally. "I am still a communist, heart and soul. Just because that Georgian lunatic betrayed that cause has not changed my views. I have fought these five years for Mother Russia, not the Soviet Union that Stalin has created. This Russia is no different from that of the Romanovs."

"Then will you help me make it so?" Dmitri took hold of his brother's shoulder urgently.

"Make it so? Dear elder brother, you babble as wildly as a drunken sailor on leave in our home town! How will you and I return Russia to Lenin's path when the Georgian madman rules with the blood-lust of the great whore, Catherine?"

Without answering, Dmitri reached inside his tunic and extracted a paper. He unfolded it and looked around him, sticking his head outside the doorway.

"What is that paper, Dmitri?"

"It's a map, little Yuri. And I got it from the same man from whom I got the uniform."

"He gave it to you?"

"After I'd killed him, yes," Dmitri replied, with a direct look at his brother.

"Good Christ, Dmitri, you killed a Colonel of the Red Army?"

"He was a Stalin supporter, Yuri. And he was very drunk one night last week. He was foolish enough to tell me his secret."

"That was enough to kill him? What is in that map?"

"It was. The map is our future, Yuri. Find us the corner of Hegelstrasse and Unter-den-Linden."

"And when we have found it?" Yuri moved out of the shelter and began to walk along the shattered ruins of the street. The soldiers had gone.

"There is a building. It was the home of a very senior officer of the Waffen SS. My late comrade who last owned this uniform told me that the honourable General had a taste for fine things.

11

They had been friends many years ago. The fine things will be stored in a safe place in that house."

"And you think they will still be there? Dmitri, much as I love and respect you, this is madness. Our troops will have looted everything by now."

"I think not, little brother. The party officials move with the army. Their fanaticism is well known. Their only job is to find Adolph Hitler and finish off the Third Reich."

Yuri was walking briskly, carrying his city map. "We have three blocks to go," he said.

The three blocks took an hour. Several times, they had to wait while armoured columns moved past them, heading for Hitler's Chancellery. At each corner they had to search the rubble to be certain it was a street junction, and to locate signs giving the road or street name. They were not always successful and dead reckoning was a large element of the navigation.

"This is the spot." Yuri spoke with confidence. Several buildings stood around them, only partially damaged. Lying in the rubble was a street sign. It said *"Hegelstrasse."* In the distance, they could see the massive swastika standing proudly atop the huge walls of Hitler's headquarters. As they watched, several cannon opened fire, aiming directly at the symbol of the Third Reich. A shell finally landed on it, exploding with a massive roar and demolishing the hated sign. A bellow of triumph issued from the thousands of men who could see the final act of contempt for the enemy, and they began to rush forward for the killing stroke.

"Quickly, this way," Dmitri snapped, consulting his paper, and moving inside the doorway of the corner building. Inside, it was dark, but both brothers took out their flashlights and studied the room.

"The stairs should be over there." Dmitri pointed his light at the far wall. They strode in the path of the beam, and found a stairwell. Descending it, the blackness became absolute, but the beams remained strong.

"Under this board, here, if the paper is correct," Dmitri said. He stamped hard at one point, and a board reared up like a startled snake. Dmitri bent down and reached inside. With a grunt of triumph, he pulled out four packages, the size of large books. "The flashlight. Here, Yuri!" he called.

In the beams of the lights, Dmitri unwrapped the four parcels. Each was a box with a hinged lid. Dmitri opened the first and played his light on the contents.

"Dear God!" Yuri whispered. The light showed the exquisite beauty of a saint's face, the gold gleaming softly with its own internal voluptuousness. "Icons!"

"The very finest, if my dead friend is correct," Dmitri muttered. "And there are six of them in two boxes. They are worth millions of American dollars."

"And in the other two?"

"Let's see," Dmitri replied and opened another lid. Inside were several soft bags drawn at their openings with a string. Dmitri pulled one open, and the flash of precious stones under the torch beams filled the gloom with beauty.

"Quickly. Get these stored in our bags," Dmitri ordered and slid his backpack from his shoulders. Yuri did the same, and a few minutes later, they re-emerged into the destruction outside.

"And now what?" Yuri asked. "How will we use these treasures to restore the dreams?"

"We have to get to America." Dmitri looked carefully around him and selected a direction. "This way, do you think?"

"Dmitri, big brother, I know you are a fine pilot and a Hero of the Soviet Union," Yuri gasped, catching up with him. "And I agree, this direction is certainly west. But we have half of Europe and an ocean to cross to reach America. And how will we just arrive?"

"I will show you soon, little brother. We have a dangerous few miles to cross, first."

"You are quite mad, Dmitri," Yuri replied. But he knew his brother's strength of will and the indomitable power that he applied to any decision. He stifled further objections and followed.

Two hours later, they had crossed two miles of the shattered capital of the dead Third Reich. The journey had been filled with fear and danger, and many times, the two brothers had hidden from Soviet troops on their final, triumphant lunge at Hitler's headquarters, or dived behind stone walls as random shells exploded around them.

Finally, Dmitri looked around him and nodded. "We are in the western sectors of the city," he said. "I recognize this part from my studies."

"And now that we are in the western sectors, what will we do?" Yuri was breathing hard in reaction from the perils of the last two hours.

"Let me show you," Dmitri replied with a slow smile. "See, over there?"

The shock hit Yuri like a physical slap. "Americans!" he gasped. "Dmitri, we must get out of here."

"No. This is perfect. They are part of the US First Division. One of General Konev's divisions met units of this division near Torgau the other day. I knew we'd see them, eventually." Not looking backward, Dmitri walked firmly toward the small group of American soldiers walking through the ruined buildings with expressions of dismay.

"Hello there." Dmitri called in English. "You must be lost." Both brothers were fluent in the language, having kept up their studies since childhood, despite the war. Dmitri had insisted.

"Jesus Christ, feller! You speak English?" The soldier who replied was a corporal. Yuri could see the rest were privates. The corporal was in charge of his six-man troop.

"Of course," Dmitri said. "I am Colonel Dmitri Alexandrovitch. This is Major Yuri Kutasov."

The American corporal seemed to think for a moment, then slowly gave a reluctant salute, returned by both brothers.

"Then can you help us, sir?" the corporal asked. "We've become split off from the rest of our squad."

"Of course, Corporal," Dmitri replied. "I saw the lines of your First Division just a little way from here. Our two army groups are already working together. If you'll follow us, we'll take you there."

"You bet, sir," the corporal replied and fell into step beside the two Russians. The expressions of relief on the faces of the young Americans were vivid, thought Yuri, wondering what his brother was up to. They had seen no Americans other than this small, lost band. Yuri looked at the two men and saw that the corporal was of a similar height and build to his brother.

"What's been happening in your sectors, sir?" the American asked.

Dmitri smiled at him. "We have been entirely successful. The Red Army took the Seelow Heights a few days ago. Last week, General Zhukov finally broke into the city, and other units took the Berlin Town Hall just two days ago. Since our armies met in Torgau, we have crushed the last remnants of these German pigs. Within the hour, we should have the Reichstag."

"That's great, sir!" The corporal and his men looked relieved. "We could be out of here in a few days."

"I'm sure of it," Dmitri replied. "Once we find the rat-hole where Hitler is hiding, it's all over and we can go home."

"Thank God." The young American exchanged grins with his men.

"Where are you from, Corporal?" Dmitri asked as they worked their way along the street.

"Los Angeles, sir."

"You come from a pleasant part of the world," Dmitri said with a smile.

"You know it, sir?" The corporal looked pleased.

"Only through your movie industry," Dmitri replied. He pointed at one of the other Americans, a tall, slender-built man. "And how about you, young man? Where are you from?"

The private gave a shy smile. "Seattle, Washington, sir." The six Americans were looking cheerful, now that they were on the way back to rejoin their fellows and talking in English with a friendly allied officer who had given them such wonderful news.

"Splendid," Dmitri replied. He looked sharply at his brother. With a shock as severe as anything caused by the explosions of this historic day, Yuri comprehended what Dmitri intended. He pulled out his pistol as Dmitri did the same, and with three precise shots in the head, killed three of the Americans before they had time to see what was happening. All six men were dead within five seconds.

The brothers shook hands amid the rubble and ruins of Berlin.

"To the New Empire," Dmitri said.

"The New Empire," Yuri replied.

A Friendly Killing

Prologue

"He'll die," said the unidentifiable voice in the phone message that the BBC had received. "And lots of other people with him. His death is for Scotland."

The voice had promised bloody mayhem. The accent was neutral, unidentifiable. The section's analysts played the tape time and time again, analysed it, dissected every vowel and consonant, every inflection, every pause. They ran the tape through electronic gizmos that drew exotic graphs on video screens, and they matched them against known speech patterns from the files. They enhanced minute background sounds to detect where the call came from, but, after all their wizardry had been expended, the experts were unhelpful.

"Scottish," they said. "Probably. Could be Aberdeen, but spent some years in the south of England. Or it could be a Sussex man who lived in Aberdeen for some years. Could even be just somebody with high mimicry skills. We're almost certain he was calling from Euston Street Station, judging by the public address system we could hear, but that's all we could determine. Difficult. Certainly not anyone we know."

So Scott went north to Edinburgh and baby-sat a large, overweight politician who had openly scoffed at Scottish nationalism and who had to attend a conference on hefty economic matters. The politician's bluster faded after the first hour, and his pale face and big, worried eyes reflected the raw fear he had so vehemently denied when the trip began.

But nothing happened.

The bomb-squads tore the conference room apart and rebuilt it, and the guards examined everyone who came in through the metal-detector bars. The dogs sniffed them, too, causing a few embarrassed giggles, but nothing caused the sharp

16

cry of havoc to sound. Scott's Browning nine-millimetre automatic remained in its shoulder holster, while his eyes tried to rip away the layers of anonymity from the faces around and see the blood-lust and killing rage, but he saw nothing. The mayhem didn't materialize. No blood was spilled over the carpets of the Edinburgh hotel. Nobody screamed in horror. Nobody died.

The absence of violence didn't alleviate Scott's nerves one bit.

"Nothing?" Jamieson's voice echoed down the line from Birmingham.

"Nothing, sir."

"And our man's gone home?"

"I've just put him safely back in his pad in Knightsbridge," Scott said. Post-mission letdown had hit him, and he was having difficulty keeping his eyes open.

"Okay. Come back, McIntyre."

"Yes, sir," Scott replied and replaced the phone.

Nothing had happened.

Dreamkill

Chapter 1

Dan Bailey died on a Thursday afternoon at five o'clock. The process was intensely uncomfortable, accompanied by vomiting, a headache like Vesuvius erupting, and a cramping of every muscle he had.

His death was watched impassively by a middle-aged man of stocky build, bald head and a flat, peasant face. As Dan went through the dreadful business, huddled up and retching in the corner of the office, all he could see of his executioner were his argyle socks above black, wingtip shoes. When it was over, the middle-aged killer called the building janitor to come and clean up the mess, pulled Dan back to his seat and gave him a drink of water from the carafe on the shelf behind the expansive executive desk. Dan sipped the water tentatively, grimacing at the acrid taste of vomit in his throat. When he had finished, when his world stopped shaking, when the cramps in his gut subsided, and when the janitor had completed his distasteful task, the man who had once been Dan Bailey stared across the desk and croaked through the pain in his temples, "Jesus Christ, Carson, just what the hell am I? And who in God's name are you?"

Ready, Steady, KILL!

Chapter 1 - Third Blood

"You think that's number three, Doc?" David Hunter looked at the horror hanging from the ceiling water pipe, fighting to keep his face expressionless.

The medical examiner stood back from the dead man. "Almost certainly," she said. "The same knife to the stomach, the same knot holding his wrists, same general type of victim, yes, I'm pretty sure you've got a serial killer on your hands, David."

"How long?"

"Initial estimate, maybe twenty to twenty-four hours. I'll tell you more after I've got him on the table. The crazy thing is that he's still got his wallet and his watch."

"So who is he, then?"

The doctor carefully opened the wallet with her surgically-gloved hands, extracted the driver's licence and read from it.

"Allan Smith," she said. "Born 5th April, 1980, address in Surry Hills, very close to here. There's about \$120 in here, various membership cards, Visa and Amex credit cards, Medicare card, some petrol receipts, so we can track some of his movements."

Hunter studied the dead man again, swallowing hard to suppress the queasiness that never failed to appear, even after fifteen years on the job and many corpses.

"About thirty," he murmured to himself. "Stripped to the waist, wrists tied with fairly common rope, hanging from the pipes just high enough so that his toes are touching the ground. Stabbed three times in the stomach, enough to kill him but not instantly. Just like the other two."

He turned back to the doctor who was stripping off her paper overalls. "How long for him to die, Angie?"

She shrugged, a look of distaste on her slender, dark face. "Probably ten, twenty minutes. Long enough to know what was happening, anyway. There are traces of sticky goo around his mouth, so I'd say his killer had stuck duct tape or something to stop him screaming. Just like the other two."

Hunter nodded at the police constable standing next to him. "Have a look around, see if you can find anything that might match."

The uniformed officer nodded and gestured to the others. The scene had already been filmed in much detail, the floor examined for footprints or other potential clues, so there was little need for caution as the new inspection started. The pool of blood beneath the body had already been washed away with a hosepipe and the car-keys uncovered by the stream taken away for analysis and identification.

"What sort of car did he drive?" Hunter asked.

"A Commodore, about three years old," replied the doctor as she packed away her equipment. "Your people checked the registration from the name and address and it matches with the driver's licence."

"Have you found it yet?"

"Not yet, but it's not anywhere close."

"So he was driven here, then," said Hunter.

"Can he go now?" asked Doctor Angela Simpson. She had finished packing away what she called her "bag of gubbins" and stood quietly, dressed in a slim-fitting pants suit in dark blue and a white shirt open at the neck. The removal of the hair cover had let her shoulder-length black hair fall free. Hunter turned to her, as always trying to suppress the small thought that she was a hell of an attractive woman and what he might do about it if she were not married to the Chief Superintendent.

"Yes," he said simply and watched as the rope was cut to allow the corpse to be lowered gently onto a stretcher, covered with a sheet and wheeled away by two young men wearing the expressionless faces of having seen too many such ugly sights. He checked that the scraps of rope were placed into plastic evidence bags for later examination by every high-tech gizmo available. He turned back to her as she spoke again.

"I'll call you as soon as I've finished," she said with a half-smile and a direct gaze into his eyes.

She knows I lust for her body, thought Hunter. *Bugger.* "Yes, please, Angie," he said aloud. "How long, do you reckon?"

She looked at her watch. "It's just after two. I might be ready by tomorrow evening. There's not a lot on, now that I've done the other two."

He nodded, avoided smiling and turned away as he heard the shout of one of the uniformed cops. *No point in encouraging her*, he thought. *Why can women always tell when a bloke's interested in them?* He walked over to the other side of the basement where the cop had called him.

"There, sir," said the young constable pointing at a screwed up scrap of grey duct tape. He had already placed a numbered post and a ruler by the spot and the photographer had taken pictures from several angles, including the distance from the point where the body had hung. Hunter picked up the scrap with his surgically-gloved hands and placed it in another plastic evidence bag. He handed it to the constable who knew what to do with it. It would be checked for prints, DNA, anything that could point to the killer.

"Okay, let's get out of here," said Detective Inspector David Hunter and walked out while the last few officers hung up the

"Scene of Crime – Do Not Enter" strips around the scene of the tragedy. Hunter felt crabby. Serial killings were bad for business. They caused panic in the city and more than the usual stress on the police. He was already exhausted from the long hours spent fruitlessly on the first and second murders and this latest one was the seal that said it really was a series. That made it several times worse as the publicity leaked out.

"Fuck it," he said aloud as he pulled away from the kerbside, and wasn't really certain whether his anger was at the killer or at the delectable, mocking and unattainable Doctor Angela Simpson.

www.ingramcontent.com/pod-product-compliance
Lightning Source LLC
Chambersburg PA
CBHW060759050426
42449CB00008B/1452